Play Activities for the Early Years

Practical Ways to Promote Purposeful Play across the Foundation Stage

Herjinder Uppal

Brilliant
PUBLICATIONS

Note

We have included publishers for all the children's books referred to in this book to enable you to get hold of them more easily. In many cases the book will have been published in a variety of formats (eg hardback and board book), sometimes by different publishers. We have not supplied publishers for traditional fairy tales (such as *The Three Little Pigs*) as there are so many versions available.

We hope you enjoy using this book. If you would like further information on other titles published by Brilliant Publications, please write to the address given below or look on our website: www.brilliantpublications.co.uk.

Other books for the Foundation Stage:

Creative Activities for the Early Years
Springtime Activities for the Early Years
Christmas Activities for the Early Years
Science and Technology for the Early Years
Games for the Early Years
Fun with Action Rhymes and Poems
Fun with Number Rhymes
Activities for 3–5 Year Olds
  All About Us
  Caring and Sharing
  Colours
  Families
  Food
  Gardening
  Pets
  Shopping
  Weather
  Water

Published by Brilliant Publications
Unit 10, Sparrow Hall Farm, Edlesborough, Dunstable, Bedfordshire LU6 2ES

website: www.brilliantpublications.co.uk

Written by Herjinder Uppal
Second edition revised and updated in 2012 by Debbie Chalmers
Illustrated by Sarah Wimperis
Cover design by Lynda Murray

Printed ISBN: 978 0 85747 671 5
ebook ISBN: 978 0 85747 672 2
© Herjinder Uppal

Printed in the UK
First published in 2004, reprinted 2010. Second edition 2012.
10 9 8 7 6 5 4 3 2 1

Contents

Introduction

Play Activities for the Early Years provides over 100 activities to guide and inspire practitioners as they support children's learning and development across all areas of the Early Years Foundation Stage (EYFS). Each activity promotes learning through play. Every unique child should be offered quality play experiences, within an enabling environment, and encouraged to form positive relationships with both adults and peers.

The new, revised *Statutory Framework for the EYFS* (from September 2012) sets the standards for learning, development and care for children from birth to five and states that the characteristics of effective learning are: Playing and exploring, Active learning and Creating and thinking critically.

The activities presented in this book can enhance children's natural eagerness to learn and progress. Becoming deeply involved in uninterrupted play for extended periods, persevering with self-chosen ideas and challenges and enjoying their experiences and achievements helps children to reach their full potential. The book will be useful to early years practitioners working in a variety of settings, such as school reception classes, nurseries, preschools, playgroups, toddler groups or as childminders.

The activity sheets can be used by practitioners for purposes such as:
- planning opportunities to offer in response to the needs and interests of individuals and groups of children
- assessment and the keeping of records, summaries and children's profiles
- guiding support staff and other adults in their participation in children's learning
- explaining the focus and the learning objectives alongside children's work and projects on display
- sharing ideas with parents and carers to enhance their understanding of their children's learning and to offer suggestions of follow-up activities that might be explored at home.

Using the activities in this book will enable practitioners to provide high quality learning opportunities and experiences for children within the Foundation Stage. While they are most suitable for those aged 30-60 months, they may be easily adapted to suit younger children, those at different developmental stages and those with individual, specific or additional needs. Each activity is linked to the appropriate Early Learning Goals from the guidance document, *Development Matters*, which indicate the level of progress that most children are expected to attain by the end of the EYFS.

The book is concise and simple to use and allows early years practitioners to plan, develop and assess day-to-day activities within their settings with confidence and enthusiasm, either by trying out each activity methodically or by dipping into them for appropriate or seasonal inspiration at any time throughout the year.

How to use this book

The *Statutory Framework for the Early Years Foundation Stage* (EYFS) sets out the Learning and Development Requirements that must shape provision in all early years settings. From September 2012, there are three prime areas and four specific areas of learning and development that are mandatory.

This book is divided into seven chapters, to cover each of these areas and its particular Early Learning Goals (ELGs).

Each chapter has a similar format and includes:

Chapter introduction

The chapter introduction describes key skills and concepts for the area of learning and development. The two or three mandatory Early Learning Goals (ELGs) for the particular prime or specific area within the Statutory Framework for the Early Years Foundation Stage (2012) are summarized, along with details of how the activities can help to encourage children to work towards the appropriate ELGs.

Table of learning opportunities

The table shows how the activities will help children to work towards, or achieve, each ELG. Where activities work towards more than one ELG and fit into more than one area, this too has been indicated. The table on pages 205–213 provides a handy summary of all the activities in the book, making it an invaluable planning tool. All the tables may be photocopied and used for planning and assessment.

Activity pages

To make the book easy to use, each activity page has a similar format, with the following headings:
- Resources – that are needed to carry out the activity
- Group size – that the activity is most suited to
- Activity – with step-by-step instructions and explanations
- Extensions – to reinforce learning, offer new challenges, extend progress and provide links to other areas of development
- Learning objectives – detailing the skills and experiences that may be acquired while engaged in the activity
- Links to Early Learning Goals – that the activity will help and encourage children to attain during the EYFS.

Many of the activities are linked to sheets that may be photocopied and used with the children to support or extend the learning opportunities. These are found immediately after the relevant activities within each chapter.

Communication and Language

The ability to understand and communicate through language affects most other areas of children's development. It allows them to express their needs, wishes, preferences and emotions, to form positive and social relationships with adults and with each other, to follow instructions and rules where necessary, to learn and find things out and to engage in satisfactory and absorbing play activities.

Children must be encouraged and supported to use language, and other ways of communicating, in a wide variety of ways: to express feelings and ideas, to give and find information, to recall the past and think about the future, and to create imaginary worlds.

The activities in this chapter help children to:
◆   communicate and use language in a variety of ways
◆   listen attentively and respond to what they hear
◆   follow instructions and make connections
◆   ask and answer questions and express themselves effectively.

There are three Early Learning Goals (ELGs) within the prime area of Communication and Language:

Listening and attention
Children listen attentively in a range of situations. They listen to stories, accurately anticipating key events and respond to what they hear with relevant comments, questions or actions. They give their attention to what others say and respond appropriately, while engaged in another activity.

Understanding
Children follow instructions involving several ideas or actions. They answer 'how' and 'why' questions about their experiences and in response to stories or events.

Speaking
Children express themselves effectively, showing awareness of listeners' needs. They use past, present and future forms accurately when talking about events that have happened or are to happen in the future. They develop their own narratives and explanations by connecting ideas or events.

The table on pages 8–9 shows which activities will help children to work towards, or achieve, these ELGs. Where an activity works towards ELGs in other areas, this has been indicated in the table.

Table of learning opportunities

Activity	Page no.	Expressive Arts and Design		Understanding the World			Mathematics		Literacy		Personal, Social and Emotional Development			Physical Development		Communication and Language		
		Being imaginative	Exploring and using media and materials	Technology	The world	People and communities	Shape, space and measures	Numbers	Writing	Reading	Making relationships	Managing feelings and behaviour	Self-confidence and self-awareness	Health and self-care	Moving and handling	Speaking	Understanding	Listening and attention
Listening area	10	✓		✓														✓
Toy telephone	11	✓														✓		
Hospital role-play	12–13	✓							✓							✓		
I spy rhyming game	14									✓							✓	✓
Picture story	15	✓														✓		✓
Number rhymes	16–17	✓														✓		✓
The wheels on the fire engine	18		✓															✓
Happy birthday	19					✓										✓		✓
Events of the day	20					✓										✓	✓	
Copy my necklace	21														✓			✓
Feely bag game	22											✓						✓
What am I doing?	23–24					✓										✓		
My friend's weekend	25				✓											✓	✓	✓
Food tasting	26				✓											✓	✓	

Play Activities for the Early Years
www.brilliantpublications.co.uk

Area	Aspect	Puppet theatre (27)	Story of the week (28)	Good manners certificate (29–30)	Pass the teddy (31)	Chocolate rice snaps cakes (32–33)	I am Goldilocks/ Baby Bear (34–36)	Book about me (37)	Diary (38)	Make a maze (39–41)
Expressive Arts and Design	Being imaginative	✓	✓				✓			✓
	Exploring and using media and materials	✓								
Understanding the World	Technology							✓		
	The world									
	People and communities									
Mathematics	Shape, space and measures									
	Numbers									
Literacy	Writing							✓	✓	
	Reading		✓			✓		✓		
Personal, Social and Emotional Development	Making relationships			✓	✓					
	Managing feelings and behaviour									
	Self-confidence and self-awareness									
Physical Development	Health and self-care									
	Moving and handling					✓		✓	✓	✓
Communication and Language	Speaking			✓		✓	✓	✓	✓	✓
	Understanding				✓	✓	✓			✓
	Listening and attention	✓	✓			✓	✓			

Listening area

Resources

A designated area specifically for the activity; CD player, tape recorder and blank cassette tapes or computer; headphones; microphones; story and song tapes and CDs with books; musical instruments; telephones; puppets.

Group size

Small groups

Activity

- Discuss with the children the idea of creating a listening area.
- Ask the children to suggest the things they would like there.
- Use these suggestions to set up the area.
- Invite the children in small groups to use the area.
- Support the children in learning how to operate the CD player and tape recorder or computer. Ensure that they understand how to record their own voices and sounds, as well as listening to recorded material.
- Provide instruments so that children can listen to themselves as they play along to songs and create different sounds.
- Invite children to use puppets to retell stories and act out different scenarios.
- Provide telephones to encourage children to talk to each other in role-play.
- Play with the children to introduce new ideas, language and vocabulary.

Learning objectives

- Listening skills, developed through a range of activities and resources
- Selecting and using equipment and technology
- Understanding and enjoyment of stories, rhymes and poems
- Creativity and imagination
- Role play – using the telephone and puppets

Extensions

- Encourage the children to share stories with each other.
- Invite children to create puppets or musical instruments and suggest that they might like to take them into the listening area. (See Puppet theatre, page 27.)
- Suggest to children that they record various sounds, both indoors and outdoors if possible, and then listen to them.
- Set up a table of objects that make noises, such as bells or wind chimes.
- Ask children to hold a shell to their ear and describe what they can hear.

Links to the Early Learning Goals

- Communication and language: Listening and attention
- Understanding the world: Technology
- Expressive arts and design: Being imaginative

Toy telephone

Resources
Paper cups; string

Group size
Whole class, then in pairs

Learning objectives
◆ Listening and speaking skills
◆ Working in pairs – cooperation and turn-taking
◆ Conversation skills
◆ How to cope in an emergency situation
◆ Social conventions and appropriate language

Activity
◆ Show children how to make a toy telephone by tying a piece of string between two cups.
◆ Invite one child to put the cup to their ear and ask another child to stand so that the string is pulled tight and talk into the cup.
◆ Encourage children to take turns to talk and to listen and to describe the sounds they hear.
◆ Discuss the things people say when they talk on the telephone, for example: 'Hello, how are you?'
◆ Talk about the different people the children talk to on the telephone (eg Dad, Mum, cousins, friends). Do they talk to each person differently?
◆ Discuss how you would use the telephone if there was an emergency. What number would you ring? How would you speak? What information would you need to supply?

◆ Invite the children to make their own telephones using paper cups and string.
◆ Encourage children to use their telephones in free play and to hold different conversations with their friends.

Extensions
◆ Play a pass the parcel game but with a telephone – the person holding the telephone when the music stops has to choose a friend to pretend to talk to on the telephone.
◆ Explain how a telephone works.
◆ Record some telephone conversations onto a tape and place them in the listening area so that the children can listen to them.

Links to the Early Learning Goals
◆ Communication and language: Speaking
◆ Expressive arts and design: Being imaginative

Hospital role-play

Resources

Role-play area set up as a hospital; labels; dressing-up outfits for doctors, nurses, paramedics, etc; toy medical kits with stethoscopes, thermometers etc; safe items from a first-aid kit such as bandages and cotton wool; note pads and pencils; toy telephones and computers.

Learning objectives

- Listening and speaking skills
- Greater understanding and confidence
- New vocabulary and language
- Mark making for a purpose

Group size

Small groups

Activity

- Invite children to play in the hospital role-play area.
- Play with the children, ensuring that adults and children take turns to be patients, doctors and other health professionals.
- Extend the children's vocabulary by introducing new words, such as 'stethoscope', 'thermometer' and 'prescription', and encouraging them to use them in their play.
- Invite the children to write out a prescription on a note pad.

Extensions

- Invite a doctor/nurse in to talk to the children or take a trip to a doctor's surgery or hospital.
- Talk about how doctors and nurses help us.
- Discuss what children should do in an emergency.
- Show the equipment in a doctor's case and talk about how it is used.
- Read *Day in the Life of a Doctor* by Linda Hayward (Dorling Kindersley Publishing).

Links to the Early Learning Goals

- Communication and language: Speaking
- Literacy: Writing
- Expressive arts and design: Being imaginative

Labels for hospital

doctor	nurse
patient	waiting room
surgery	receptionist
medicine	stethoscope
plasters	bandage
thermometer	x-ray

I spy rhyming game

Resources
Flip chart and pens

Group size
Whole class

Learning objectives
◆ Listening and speaking skills
◆ The ability to recognize and use rhyme

Activity
◆ Initiate and lead a group discussion about rhyme, inviting children to contribute ideas. Write down some of the words that the children think of and read them aloud, emphasizing the rhymes.
◆ Now discuss how the I spy rhyming game is played – instead of saying, 'I spy something beginning with (a letter), the person has to say, 'I spy something that rhymes with (a word).'
◆ Play the I spy rhyming game.
◆ Let children have turns at guessing and asking.

Extensions
◆ Make an I spy rhyming flap book.
◆ Read some nursery rhymes and ask children to make up their own rhymes.
◆ Invite the group to find as many words as possible that rhyme with a simple, regular, familiar word, such as 'cat'.
◆ Make up a class poem using rhyming.

Links to the Early Learning Goals
◆ Communication and language: Listening and attention, Understanding
◆ Literacy: Reading

Picture story

Resources
Pictures of different objects or actions

Group size
Large groups

Learning objectives
◆ Listening and speaking skills
◆ Using language patterns and developing narratives
◆ Presenting ideas to others
◆ Creativity and imagination

Activity
◆ Invite a group of children to sit together in a circle and place a collection of pictures in the middle.
◆ Explain to the children that they could make up a group story if each child adds an idea in turn, using a picture as a guide.
◆ Start the story when a child picks up a picture and offers an opening phrase or sentence. Encourage another child to pick up a different picture and continue the story. Ask questions or offer suggestions if any children struggle to think of a contribution when it is their turn.
◆ Continue until all the children have had a turn and the last child finishes the story.
◆ Now shuffle the pictures and start again.

Extensions
◆ Write down or record the stories.
◆ Instead of picture cards you could use objects.
◆ Make up a poem using the picture cards.
◆ Ask children to make their own picture cards by using small pieces of card and pictures cut out of magazines.
◆ Make picture cards to represent scenes and events within a familiar story, shuffle them and encourage children to place them in a sequence that tells the story in the correct order.

Links to the Early Learning Goals
◆ Communication and language: Listening and attention, Speaking
◆ Expressive arts and design: Being imaginative

Nursery rhymes

Resources
Teddy bear; mixed up nursery rhymes sheet (see page 17); scissors; glue; paper

Group size
Whole class, then small groups

Learning objectives
- Listening and speaking skills
- Understanding language patterns, rhymes and sequences
- Learning popular rhymes to use confidently in play and group interactions

Activity
- Discuss which nursery rhymes the children are familiar with and which they like best. Say or sing them together.
- Show the children the teddy bear and explain that the only person who can speak is the person holding the teddy.
- Say the first line of a nursery rhyme while holding the teddy, then pass it to a child and ask whether they can say the next line. The child can then pass the teddy on again, with each person saying a line while holding it, until the end of the rhyme is reached.
- Show the children the sheet of nursery rhyme pictures which are in the wrong order.
- Ask them to cut out the pictures and arrange them in the right order.
- Stick the pictures onto paper.
- Finish the activity by letting the children share their work with the class and recite the rhyme.

Extensions
- Provide a selection of dressing up clothes and props, so that the children may act out popular rhymes and role-play situations.
- Make a book about the children's favourite nursery rhymes.
- Find out the children's favourite nursery rhymes and make a bar chart together.
- Use puppets to act out rhymes.

Links to the Early Learning Goals
- Communication and language: Listening and attention, Speaking
- Expressive arts and design: Being imaginative

Mixed up nursery rhymes sheet

Hey Diddle Diddle

Hickory Dickory Dock

Jack and Jill

The wheels on the fire engine

Resources
Flip chart and pen; tape recorder and blank cassette tape or computer and microphone

Group size
Whole class

Learning objectives
- Listening and speaking skills
- Understanding language patterns, rhymes and sequences
- Learning popular rhymes to use confidently in play and group interactions
- Recognising everyday sounds

Activity
- Sing the song 'The Wheels On The Bus' with the children.
- Suggest that the song could be changed to involve a fire engine instead and ask children to make suggestions, thinking of the different parts of a fire engine and the sounds they make. For example, you might come up with: horn (beep, beep), hose pipe (whoosh, whoosh), ladder (up and down), siren (nee, naw).
- Write the children's ideas on the flip chart.
- Now sing the song again but with the new words.
- Finish by recording the song and placing it in the listening area for all to enjoy.

Extensions
- Create other variations involving other vehicles, such as a bicycle, a truck or an ambulance.
- Adapt other popular songs.
- Sing and listen to other songs and make a recording to play in the listening area.
- Make a bus or fire engine using cardboard boxes, chairs, etc.
- Talk about what children should do if there is a fire at school/preschool/nursery.
- Go for a trip to a fire station or invite firefighters to visit the setting.

Links to the Early Learning Goals
- Communication and language: Listening and attention
- Expressive arts and design: Exploring and using media and materials

Play Activities for the Early Years
www.brilliantpublications.co.uk

Happy birthday

Resources
Birthday cards; book: *Kipper's Birthday* by Mike Inkpen (Hodder Headline Ltd)

Group size
Large groups

Learning objectives
◆ Listening to stories with increasing attention and recall
◆ Responding to questions and discussion with relevant comments based on own experiences
◆ Expressing ideas and explanations of events effectively, showing an awareness of listeners and using past, present and future forms
◆ Understanding similarities and differences between families, communities and traditions

Activity
◆ Read the story *Kipper's Birthday*.
◆ Use the book as a stimulus to talk to the children about birthdays.
◆ Show the children some birthday cards.
◆ Invite the children to take turns to describe how they celebrated their last birthday.
◆ Ask questions to encourage the children to talk as much as they can on the topic.

Extensions
◆ Ask the children to make birthday cards for Kipper.
◆ Ask the children to draw a cake with the right number of candles for their age.
◆ Make a list of all the children's birthdays in each month.
◆ Make a bar chart using the list of children's birthdays in each month.
◆ For each child's birthday give a card and have a small celebration.
◆ Cook small birthday cakes.

Links to the Early Learning Goals
◆ Communication and language: Listening and attention, Speaking
◆ Understanding the world: People and communities

Events of the day

Resources

Photographs of children engaged in activities at particular times of the day; paper; glue

Group size

Small groups

Activity

- ◆ Show the children photos of the class doing different things during the day, for example arriving and taking off coats, snack time, etc.
- ❖ Ask the children to sort out the pictures and put them in the right order.
- ◆ Stick the pictures onto a large sheet of paper.
- ◆ Ask the group to show their work to the class and talk about the different events in the day.

Extensions

- ◆ Ask children to talk about the things they did at the weekend starting on Saturday morning and finishing on Sunday evening.

- ◆ Give children pictures of activities they do in the morning (eg get out of bed, brush their teeth, eat breakfast). Ask the children to put the pictures in the correct sequence.
- ◆ Initiate a discussion on time. Decide with the children which activities happen at specific points during a day, eg What time do we have a snack? Talk about activities which can happen at any time, eg When do we read stories or play in the garden?
- ◆ Learn the days of the week and the months of the year.
- ◆ Give the children pictures of a story or nursery rhyme they know well. Ask them to put the pictures in the correct order (see Nursery rhymes, pages 16–17).

Links to the Early Learning Goals
- ☐ Communication and language: Understanding, Speaking
- ☐ Understanding the world: People and communities

Copy my necklace

Resources
Keys, rings, beads and buttons of different shapes and colours (two of each); string; large piece of thick card

Group size
Pairs

Learning objectives
◆ Listening carefully, asking questions and following instructions
◆ Fine motor control – threading

Activity
◆ Use the card to form a screen between two children who are seated at a table, so that they cannot see each other.
◆ Give each child a string and one of each of the items. For younger children limit the number of items.
◆ Tie a knot in the end of a piece of string and invite one of the children to thread objects onto the string in any order.
◆ Ask the child with the necklace to give instructions to the other child so that they put objects on their necklace in the same sequence. For example, 'Put the key on first, now put on the yellow, round bead.'
◆ The other child can ask questions to check they are following the instructions correctly.
◆ When finished remove the screen and compare the necklaces.

Extensions
◆ Use the same technique for other activities, for example making models, pictures, etc.
◆ Blindfold one child and ask another child to give directions so that the child can walk from one side of the classroom to the other safely.
◆ Pretend one child is a robot and another child has to give it instructions to do a certain activity (see Robot game, page 153).
◆ Play games in which the children have to listen carefully, such as Simon says.

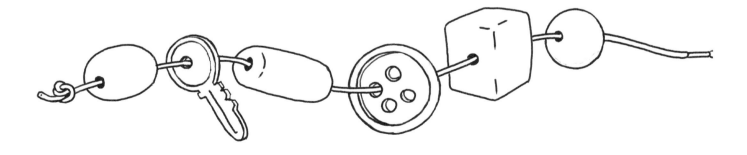

Links to the Early Learning Goals
◆ Communication and language: Understanding
◆ Physical development: Moving and handling

Feely bag game

Resources
Large bag; different objects (eg teddy bear, keys, cup, book, iron and pen)

Group size
Large groups

Activity
◆ Place an object in the bag without the children seeing.
◆ Explain to the children that they are going to take turns to guess what an object is by just feeling it. Explain that they should not tell anyone what they think the object is.
◆ In order to play the game, the other children have to ask questions to find out what the object is. For example, 'Is it small?' 'Is it used in the house?' The child with the bag can answer only 'yes' or 'no'.
◆ Limit the children to 10 questions.
◆ Encourage the children to listen carefully to each other's answers to help them ask their next question.
◆ Finish by asking the children to guess what the object is. Check to see if they are correct.
◆ Ensure that every child who wishes to may take a turn at feeling the object in the bag and both asking and answering the questions.

Learning objective
◆ The ability to ask and answer questions effectively
◆ Listening and concentration skills
◆ The ability to learn through touch and tactile experiences

Extensions
◆ Play a yes/no game. One child pretends to be someone famous and the other children have to ask questions to guess who they are.
◆ Play Chinese whispers. See if the message at the end is the same as the one at the beginning.
◆ Play card games such as Patience or Snap to build concentration.
◆ Invite a speaker in (according to the topic of the term). Ask the children to be respectful and listen carefully. Encourage them to think of and ask relevant questions.

Links to the Early Learning Goals
◆ Communication and language: Listening and attention
◆ Understanding the world: The world

What am I doing?

Resources
What am I doing? sheet (see page 24)

Group size
Large groups

Activity
◆ Show the children the What am I doing? sheet. Discuss the various activities shown.
◆ Explain to the children that you are going to act out one of the activities and you want them to guess what you are doing.
◆ Now ask the child who guessed correctly to choose a different activity from the sheet and to act it out for the others to guess.
◆ Carry on until all the children have had a turn at miming.

Learning objectives
◆ Different ways of communicating
◆ Gross motor control – to use the body to convey information
◆ Group cooperation and taking turns fairly

Extensions
◆ Ask children to make facial expressions to convey how they are feeling.
◆ Play Chinese whispers, but instead of a whisper, pass round a gesture such as a wink or a pat on the back.
◆ Ask the children to use puppets to retell a story. (See Puppet theatre, page 27.)
◆ Show the children a collection of different foods. Ask one child to mime eating one of the foods for the other children to guess which one they are eating.
◆ Give the children a safety mirror and ask them to make different facial expressions.

Links to the Early Learning Goals
◆ Communication and language: Listening and attention, Speaking
◆ Personal, social and emotional development: Managing feelings and behaviour

What am I doing? sheet

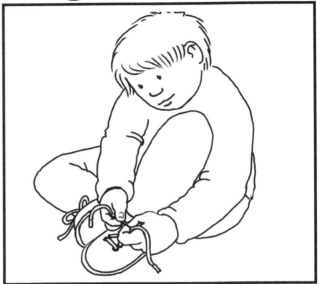

Play Activities for the Early Years
www.brilliantpublications.co.uk

My friend's weekend

Resources
No special requirements

Group size
Pairs

Activity
◆ Ask the children to sit in pairs facing each other.
◆ Explain to the children that you would like them to talk to one another about the things they did that weekend.
◆ Point out that they only have a minute each to talk and find out as much information as possible. Encourage the children to question their partner to get as much information as possible.
◆ Once they have finished ask each child to report back what their partner did.

Learning objectives
◆ Collaboration and cooperation skills
◆ Listening and speaking skills
◆ Understanding, remembering and delivering information

Extensions
◆ Ask the children to talk to each other about different topics, for example their family or their favourite holiday.
◆ Invite children to share a book with a partner (eg an older child or adult).
◆ Ask children to copy each other's body movements.
◆ Provide musical instruments. Ask one child to play a sound pattern for the other child to copy.

Links to Early Learning Goals
◆ Communication and language: Listening and attention, Speaking
◆ Understanding the world: People and communities

Food tasting

Resources
A variety of food (jelly, sweets, lemon, noodles, apple, samosas, yoghurt)

Group size
Small groups

Learning objectives
- New vocabulary to describe various tastes and textures
- Recognizing salty, spicy or sweet foods
- Experiencing foods from different countries

Activity
- Be aware of children's allergies, intolerances and dietary requirements when choosing foods to be tasted.
- Show the children a wide range of food.
- Invite the children to taste one of the foods, for example, the jelly.
- Ask the children to describe how it feels in their mouth and also how it tastes.
- Do the same with the other food items.
- Model language by tasting some food yourself. For example, if you are eating a samosa you might say, 'It tastes spicy and it feels crunchy in my mouth.'

Extension
- Blindfold the children. Does it make a difference to how the foods taste?
- Cook food for tasting.
- Learn about the different areas of the tongue. There are only four different flavours we can taste – sour, salty, bitter and sweet. The front of the tongue tastes sweet flavours, the sides taste sour and the back is for bitter flavours. Salty flavours can be tasted all over the mouth.
- Have an international food day. Ask children to taste food from around the world (see International food, page 183).
- Make a bar chart of the children's favourite foods.

Links to the Early Learning Goals
- Communication and language: Understanding, Speaking
- Understanding the world: The world

Puppet theatre

Resources

Book: *The Three Little Pigs*; chairs and blanket (for puppet theatre); old socks; felt-tip pens; pipe cleaners; felt; wool; fabric pieces; buttons; glue

Group size

Large groups

Learning objectives

◆ Creativity and imagination in art work
◆ Remembering and retelling stories
◆ Confidence in character acting and performance

Activity

◆ Begin by reading the story *The Three Little Pigs*.
◆ Explain to the children that they are going to make puppets of the characters in the story (eg the three pigs, the people that sell straw, sticks and bricks, and the wolf).
◆ Give the children the resources and let them create the puppets themselves.
◆ Set up a puppet theatre by draping the blanket over some chairs. The children can then hide behind the blanket and raise their hands so that the audience can see the puppets.
◆ Explain to the children that they are going to retell the story using the puppets.
◆ Encourage the children to create different character voices to use with different puppets.
◆ Support the groups of children in performing their puppet plays to each other.

Extensions

◆ If possible, go to see a puppet show or invite a puppet show to the setting. This will give the children lots of ideas and also inspire them.
◆ Talk about the different ways and different resources used to make puppets.
◆ Use a puppet to represent one character from the story. Ask children to retell the story from that character's point of view. For example, the wolf might say: 'I was just so hungry but the pig wouldn't let me in.'
◆ Make puppets to go with other stories.
◆ Plan a birthday party for your puppets, then hold the party.
◆ Hide a puppet and give directions to a child to find it.
◆ Look at puppets from around the world.

Links to the Early Learning Goals

◆ Communication and language: Listening and attention
◆ Expressive arts and design: Exploring and using media and materials, Being imaginative

Story of the week

Resources
Storybook; dressing-up clothes and props

Group size
Whole class, then small groups

Learning objectives
◆ Remembering and retelling stories
◆ Confidence in character acting and performance

Activity
◆ Choose a story of the week.
◆ Read the story out a few times over the week. Hopefully by the end of the week the children will be able to read it with you.
◆ When the children are familiar with the story, pause at different stages when reading the book and ask the children what happens next.
◆ Invite individual children to retell parts of the story to the rest of the group.
◆ Set up a display of the book and some dressing-up clothes and props.
◆ Invite children to act out the story, using the clothes and props, during free play.
◆ Make a wall display about the book and other activities based on it.

Extensions
◆ Read a big book version of the story.
◆ Make some props to go with the story.
◆ Support children in making puppets that they would like to use in retelling and acting out the story.
◆ Write and display some of the key words used in the story for children to recognize and read.
◆ Make a magnetic story board with pictures of the characters (place a self-adhesive magnetic strip on the back of the pictures). Ask children to retell the story using the pictures.

Links to the Early Learning Goals
◆ Communication and language: Listening and attention
◆ Literacy: Reading
◆ Expressive arts and design: Being imaginative

Good manners certificate

Resources
Good manners certificate (see page 30); chart with children's names on it; star stickers

Group size
Whole class

Learning objectives
◆ Polite, sensitive and confident speech
◆ Listening to, respecting and empathizing with others
◆ Developing positive relationships and a positive atmosphere in the setting

Activity
◆ Talk to the children about how to demonstrate good manners, for example saying 'please' and 'thank you'.
◆ Ask the children to give examples of how they could use good manners, for example listening to others or talking politely.
◆ Explain to the children that they may stick a star next to their name when an adult notices that they are using good speaking or listening skills. Children who collect more than a certain number of stars during a week may receive a certificate.
◆ Award certificates to children who have earned enough stars during the last session they attend each week.

Extensions
◆ Instead of giving out certificates, adults could display photographs of the children who have earned several stars in a particular place.
◆ Invite some people to talk to the group. Talk with the children in advance about how they should greet the speakers and how to speak to them.
◆ Provide toy telephones in the role-play area and model pretend conversations to encourage the children to use them (see Toy telephone, page 11). Discuss the different people they might talk to and how they can be polite.
◆ Make a list of good manners with the children. (See Golden rules, page 78.)
◆ Read, tell or make up a story about children who had bad manners and what happened to them.
◆ Read the story *The Bad-Tempered Ladybird* by Eric Carle (Puffin Books).

Links to the Early Learning Goals
◆ Communication and language: Speaking
◆ Personal, social and emotional development: Making relationships

Good manners certificate

This certificate
is presented to

_____

for being a good talker
and listener.

Well done!

Play Activities for the Early Years
www.brilliantpublications.co.uk

Pass the teddy

Resources
Teddy bear

Group size
Small groups

Activity
◆ Ask the children to sit in a circle.
◆ Explain to the children that they are going to play a game to show they remember their friends' names.
◆ You hold the teddy and say, 'I am (your name).' Then pass the teddy to the child sitting next to you, saying, 'Hello (child's name), please will you look after the teddy?'
◆ The child takes the teddy and says, 'Thank you, (sender's name), of course I will look after it.' They then continue with, 'I am (name),' before passing the teddy to the next child and inviting them to look after it, as before.
◆ Continue around the circle until the teddy is back to you.

Extensions
◆ Ask children to bring toys from home. Ask the children to swap toys. Have the children start by saying, 'I am (name), this is my toy.' Then swap it with a friend whist saying '(name of child) please will you look after my toy?' (See My favourite toy, page 71.)
◆ Do the same activity but use a ball which they can roll to the person of their choice.
◆ Invite speakers to the classroom. Remind the children that they need to talk politely and clearly.

Links to the Early Learning Goals
◆ Communication and language: Speaking
◆ Personal, social and emotional development: Making relationships

Chocolate rice snaps cakes

Resources
Chocolate rice snaps cakes recipe and ingredients (see page 33); aprons

Group size
Small groups

Learning objectives
◆ Understanding that information can be relayed in print
◆ Following instructions and pictorial clues
◆ Basic cookery skills and using equipment effectively
◆ Linking reading with mathematics and science

Activity
◆ Start by asking children to wash their hands and put on an apron.
◆ Give each child a copy of the recipe sheet and read through it with them.
◆ Explain to the children that they are going to make the cakes by following the recipe one step at a time.
◆ Give each child a bowl and spoon and help them go through the recipe.
◆ Explain to the children that the pictures will help them to understand what they have to do at each step.
◆ Finish by letting everyone enjoy the cakes.

Extensions
◆ Try other simple recipes.
◆ Make a class recipe book.
◆ Invite the children to make up a magic recipe, for example, a recipe for sweets that make you invisible.
◆ Follow sets of instructions for other activities.
◆ Look at instruction manuals.
◆ Look at other pieces of writing that provide information: posters, bus/train timetables, menus, dress patterns, etc.

Links to the Early Learning Goals
◆ Communication and language: Listening and attention, Understanding
◆ Physical development: Moving and handling
◆ Literacy: Reading

Chocolate rice snaps cakes recipe

Ingredients
2 chocolate bars
box of rice snaps cereal
cup
teaspoon

Resources
mixing spoon
bowl
paper cake cases
fridge

Activity
Melt the chocolate. Let it cool.
Give each child a bowl and a mixing spoon.

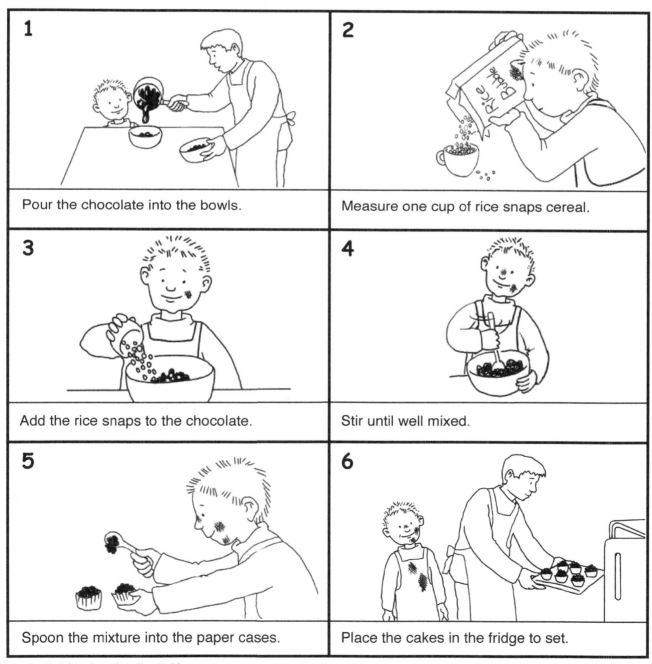

1	2
Pour the chocolate into the bowls.	Measure one cup of rice snaps cereal.
3	4
Add the rice snaps to the chocolate.	Stir until well mixed.
5	6
Spoon the mixture into the paper cases.	Place the cakes in the fridge to set.

I am Goldilocks / Baby Bear

Resources
Book: *Goldilocks and the Three Bears*; Goldilocks mask (see page 35); Baby Bear mask (see page 36). Photocopy masks onto card and attach to lolly sticks.

Group size
Large groups

Activity
◆ Begin by reading the story *Goldilocks and the Three Bears*.
◆ Discuss how Goldilocks must have felt. Ask the children how they think she felt when she entered the house, and when she saw the three bears.
◆ Discuss how Baby Bear must have felt. Ask the children if they think that he was happy when he was walking in the forest, and how they think he felt when he saw that his chair was broken.
◆ Show the children the masks.
◆ Now ask one child to put on the Goldilocks mask and tell the story as Goldilocks would have told it. For example, 'One day I was going for a walk in the woods when I saw a house. I went in the house and saw three bowls of porridge.'
◆ Now ask another child to put on the Baby Bear mask and tell the story as Baby Bear would. For example, 'One morning I woke up and Mum had made porridge for breakfast. It was too hot so Mum, Dad and I went for a walk.'
◆ The children might find this difficult to do so model the task for them to help give them ideas.
◆ Finish by leaving the masks in the dressing-up area for children to act out the story during free play.

Learning objectives
◆ Understanding the structure of a story
◆ Remembering stories and retelling them from different perspectives
◆ Character acting and dialogues
◆ Expressing thoughts, feelings and emotions

Extensions
◆ Make costumes to go with the masks.
◆ Retell the story from Mummy Bear's and Daddy Bear's perspective.
◆ Discuss how Goldilocks was wrong to go into a stranger's house. Talk about safety.
◆ Link similar activities to other traditional stories, such as *The Three Little Pigs*. Make appropriate masks.
◆ Write stories from the perspective of different characters.

Links to the Early Learning Goals
◆ Communication and language: Listening and attention, Understanding, Speaking
◆ Expressive arts and design: Being imaginative

Goldilocks mask

Baby Bear mask

Play Activities for the Early Years
www.brilliantpublications.co.uk

Book about me

Resources

Scrap book; photos of children with their families (provided by children); pencils; felt-tip pens

Group size

Large groups

Learning objectives

◆ Understanding that information can be found in books
◆ Forming positive images of themselves and their peers
◆ Attempting to read and write simple words and sentences

Activity

◆ Explain to children that they are going to make an information book about themselves.
◆ Point out that books that provide information are called non-fiction books.
◆ Give each child a scrap book and ask them to bring in some photos of themselves and their families.
◆ Ask them to write simple sentences using words they know. Encourage them to attempt to write any words they do not know by using letter sounds.
◆ Allow them to work as independently as possible.
◆ Act as a scribe for children who are less confident.
◆ Finish by letting the children swap books with each other so they can learn about each other.
◆ Put the books in the book corner.

Extensions

◆ Ask children to make a book about their best friend. They must first interview their friend to get the information they need.
◆ Read a variety of non-fiction books and point out the contents and index pages.
◆ Invite the children to use a computer to type up their work.
◆ Give children a pile of books and ask them to sort them into fiction and non-fiction.
◆ Ask children to sight read some words. Cover up the words and ask the children to try to write the words using their memory and knowledge of phonics.

Links to the Early Learning Goals

◆ Communication and language: Understanding, Speaking
◆ Physical development: Moving and handling
◆ Literacy: Reading, Writing
◆ Understanding the world: Technology

Diary

Resources
Flip chart and pen; exercise books; pencils

Group size
Whole class

Learning objectives
◆ Listening and speaking within a familiar large group
◆ Using phonic knowledge to aid independent writing
◆ Beginning to understand basic punctuation

Activity
◆ Try to include this activity each Monday morning. If not all of the children in the setting attend every day, consider providing it separately for small groups on the first days of the week that they attend.
◆ Invite children to come together as a group and discuss how they spent their weekend.
◆ Whilst they talk, write some of their sentences on a flip chart, using punctuation.
◆ Give each child a diary book.
◆ Invite the children to draw a picture and write one sentence about their weekend in their diary book.
◆ Act as a scribe where necessary.
◆ Encourage them to write words they know and also to use their knowledge of letter sounds to try to write more complex words.
◆ Remind children to use punctuation – capital letter at the beginning and a full stop at the end.
◆ Finish with some children reading out their work.

Extensions
◆ Invite some children to type their sentences on a computer.
◆ Pair up children and ask them to write about each other's weekend rather than their own.
◆ Have a display of common words to help children in their writing.
◆ Ask children to make up an imaginary story about their weekend. For example, 'I went on a flying carpet to Disneyland.' Record the stories or scribe for the children.
◆ Write a sentence for each day of the week. For example, 'On Monday I played football. On Tuesday I wrote a story. On Wednesday….'
◆ Learn the days of the week.

Links to the Early Learning Goals
◆ Communication and language: Speaking
◆ Physical development: Moving and handling
◆ Literacy: Writing

Make a maze

Resources
Pictures of mazes; Mazes 1 and 2 (see pages 40 – 41); chairs; tables; boxes; large pieces of card; string; rope; hoops; pencil and paper to draw maze

Group size
Large groups

Learning objectives
◆ Listening and speaking skills
◆ Giving, responding to and following instructions
◆ Planning and problem-solving skills
◆ Creativity and imagination
◆ Directions, such as forward and backward, left and right

Activity
◆ Begin by showing pictures of mazes and the Mazes sheets. Explain that the aim is to travel from one end of the maze to the other.
◆ Ask the children to solve the mazes on the sheets.
◆ Show the children the equipment that is available and and support them as they plan to make their own maze.
◆ Draw the plan on a large sheet of paper.
◆ Now help children to construct the maze by looking at the plan. Encourage them to adapt their plan if they come across any difficulties.
◆ Finally let children play in the maze and time how quickly they can complete it.

Extensions
◆ Add things to make the maze more challenging. For example, children could be asked to complete the maze whilst balancing a bean bag on their head.
◆ If possible take a trip to a maze.
◆ Design and make an obstacle course (see Obstacle course, page 154).
◆ Draw some mazes on paper for others to solve.
◆ Suggest to the children that they work in pairs, with one child pretending to be a robot and the other child giving directions to the robot to complete the maze.

Links to the Early Learning Goals
◆ Communication and language: Understanding, Speaking
◆ Physical development: Moving and handling
◆ Expressive arts and design: Being imaginative

Maze 1

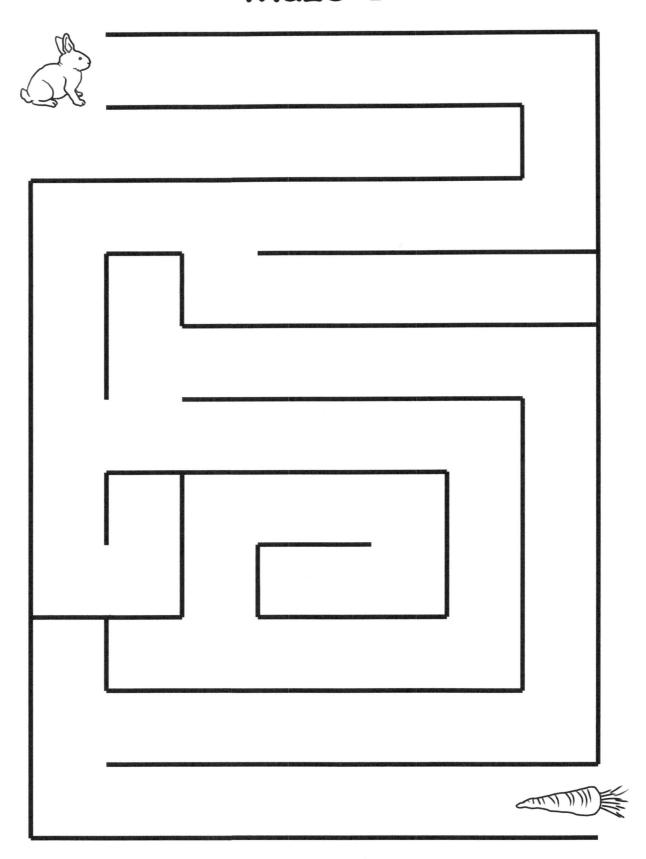

Play Activities for the Early Years
www.brilliantpublications.co.uk

Maze 2

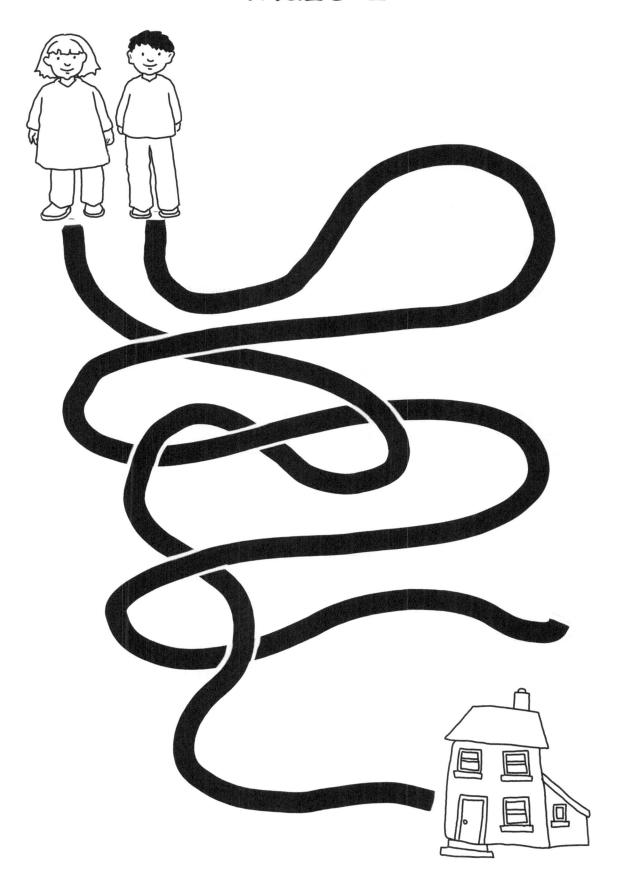

Physical Development

Practitioners know that children need to gain knowledge and understanding of their own bodies in order to build confidence in themselves, to accept challenges and risks and to find satisfaction in physical games and tasks.

Children must be encouraged and supported to develop greater control and coordination through practising movements and using tools and equipment. They must also have opportunities to learn about healthy diet and exercise, basic hygiene and personal needs and how to keep themselves and others safe.

The activities in this chapter help children to:
◆ develop greater control and coordination in large and small movements
◆ increase physical fitness, strength and stamina
◆ gain knowledge about their own bodies, personal needs, health and safety
◆ negotiate space confidently and safely
◆ become confident to try new skills and challenging tasks.

There are two Early Learning Goals (ELGs) within the prime area of Physical Development:

Moving and handling
Children show good control and coordination in large and small movements. They move confidently in a range of ways, safely negotiating space. They handle equipment and tools effectively, including pencils for writing.

Health and self-care
Children know the importance for good health of physical exercise, and a healthy diet, and talk about ways to keep healthy and safe. They manage their own basic hygiene and personal needs successfully, including dressing and going to the toilet independently.

The table on pages 43–44 shows which activities will help children to work towards, or achieve, these ELGs. Where an activity works towards ELGs in other areas, this has been indicated in the table.

Table of learning opportunities

Activity	Page no.	Being imaginative	Exploring and using media and materials	Technology	The world	People and communities	Shape, space and measures	Numbers	Writing	Reading	Making relationships	Managing feelings and behaviour	Self-confidence and self-awareness	Health and self-care	Moving and handling	Speaking	Understanding	Listening and attention
Chopstick challenge	45							✓							✓		✓	
Picnic food	46	✓	✓								✓				✓			
Mini-beast safari	47	✓					✓	✓			✓				✓		✓	✓
Beanbag games	48	✓									✓				✓		✓	✓
Trolley dash	49										✓				✓		✓	✓
Traffic light game	50										✓			✓	✓		✓	✓
Skittle fun	51							✓			✓				✓		✓	
Easy catch	52							✓			✓				✓		✓	
Musical cushions	53							✓			✓				✓		✓	✓
Relation time	54													✓	✓		✓	✓
Is it healthy?	55													✓	✓	✓	✓	✓
Healthy teeth	56–57													✓	✓	✓	✓	✓

Column groupings:
- Expressive Arts and Design: Being imaginative; Exploring and using media and materials
- Understanding the World: Technology; The world; People and communities
- Mathematics: Shape, space and measures; Numbers
- Literacy: Writing; Reading
- Personal, Social and Emotional Development: Making relationships; Managing feelings and behaviour; Self-confidence and self-awareness
- Physical Development: Health and self-care; Moving and handling
- Communication and Language: Speaking; Understanding; Listening and attention

Activity	Page no.	Listening and attention	Understanding	Speaking	Moving and handling	Health and self-care	Self-confidence and self-awareness	Managing feelings and behaviour	Making relationships	Reading	Writing	Numbers	Shape, space and measures	People and communities	The world	Technology	Exploring and using media and materials	Being imaginative
Healthy food plate	58	✓		✓	✓	✓												
Going on a Bear Hunt	59	✓		✓	✓													✓
Grand Old Duke of York	60				✓				✓								✓	✓
Clay pot	61		✓		✓							✓					✓	
Papier mâché ladybirds	62		✓		✓				✓			✓			✓		✓	

Column area groupings:
- Communication and Language: Listening and attention, Understanding, Speaking
- Physical Development: Moving and handling, Health and self-care
- Personal, Social and Emotional Development: Self-confidence and self-awareness, Managing feelings and behaviour, Making relationships
- Literacy: Writing, Reading
- Mathematics: Numbers, Shape, space and measures
- Understanding the World: Technology, The world, People and communities
- Expressive Arts and Design: Being imaginative, Exploring and using media and materials

Play Activities for the Early Years
www.brilliantpublications.co.uk

Chopstick challenge

Resources
Chopsticks or tweezers; small objects (buttons, beads, erasers, small world toys); pots; sand timer

Group size
Small groups

Learning objectives
◆ Fine motor skills while handling equipment and tools
◆ Control and hand–eye coordination in small movements
◆ Concentration and responding to and following instructions
◆ Counting skills

Activity
◆ Lay out some small objects on a flat surface.
◆ Give each child a small pot and some chopsticks or tweezers.
◆ Show children how to use the chopsticks using a tripod grip.
◆ Explain to children that you are going to give them a challenge. The challenge is to pick up as many items as they can using the chopsticks before the sand timer finishes.
◆ Start the sand timer. Help the children to hold the chopsticks correctly.
◆ Count how many items each child has collected.

Extensions
◆ Cook some noodles and ask children to try to eat them using the chopsticks.
◆ Put glue onto a picture and then sprinkle on some glitter or sand using a finger–thumb grip.
◆ Thread beads onto laces.
◆ Draw pictures or patterns using different tools, such as chalk, cotton buds, feathers.

Links to the Early Learning Goals
◆ Physical development: Moving and handling
◆ Communication and language: Understanding
◆ Mathematics: Numbers

Picnic food

Resources
Blanket; toys; playdough; playdough tools (cutters, blunt knives, spatulas, etc)

Group size
Large groups

Learning objectives
- Using a range of materials and tools
- Fine motor skills
- Creativity and imagination
- Social and cooperative play, taking turns and sharing
- Exploring shapes, colours and textures

Activity
- Explain to the children that they are going to have a picnic with their toys, but first they need to make some pretend food with playdough.
- Ask the children to suggest the food they would like to have on the picnic. Write a list.
- Now go through the list and talk about each food: the shape, size, texture, etc. Talk about how they could make the food with playdough. For example, to make sausages they could roll out the playdough using the palm of their hand.
- Invite the children to make the different food with the playdough using the tools provided.
- Finish by spreading out the blanket and letting the children have a pretend picnic with their toys.

Extensions
- Make food out of other materials: Plasticine, clay, etc.
- Count how many toys there are and how much food is needed.
- Sort food into hoops according to shape, colour and type.
- Make a list with the children of the food they would like to have at their picnic.
- Make some real picnic food and go on a real picnic.

Links to the Early Learning Goals
- Physical development: Moving and handling
- Personal, social and emotional development: Making relationships
- Expressive arts and design: Exploring and using media and materials, Being imaginative

Mini-beast safari

Resources
Books, CD Roms and DVDs; pictures of mini-beasts

Group size
Whole class

Learning objective
◆ Control and coordination in whole body movements
◆ Creative and imaginative movement and role-play
◆ Following instructions in order to participate in group games and activities
◆ Interacting and cooperating with others
◆ Awareness and understanding of names and features of various mini-beasts

Activity
◆ Show the children the information about different mini-beasts.
◆ Discuss with them how different mini-beasts move around:
  ❖ spiders – scurry around very quickly
  ❖ butterflies – fly gracefully
  ❖ bees – buzz from one flower to the next
  ❖ ants – march in a line
  ❖ worms – wiggle through the earth
  ❖ grasshoppers – leap around.
◆ Invite the children to play a game involving moving around as the different mini-beasts, changing as the different names are called out. For example, if they hear 'butterfly', they should fly gracefully from one flower to the next; if they hear 'spider', they should mime the spinning of a web.
◆ Try another game involving children in taking turns to pretend to be mini-beasts while the others try to guess which ones they are.

Extensions
◆ Ask the children to make costumes of mini-beasts and have a mini-beast party.
◆ Look for and observe mini-beasts in the garden.
◆ Make different mini-beasts out of playdough.
◆ Count the number of legs each mini-beast has.
◆ Sort plastic mini-beasts into hoops: by colour, number of legs, etc.

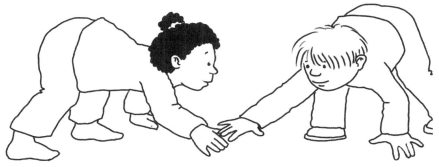

Links to the Early Learning Goals
◆ Physical development: Moving and handling
◆ Communication and language: Listening and attention, Understanding
◆ Personal, social and emotional development: Making relationships
◆ Mathematics: Numbers, Shape, space and measures
◆ Expressive arts and design: Being imaginative

Beanbag games

Resources

Beanbags; skittles; hoop; bucket; obstacle course equipment

Group size

Whole class

Learning objectives

- ◆ Control and coordination in large and small movements
- ◆ Confidence in handling and balancing equipment
- ◆ Following instructions in order to participate in group games and activities
- ◆ Interacting and cooperating with others

Activity

- ◆ Explain to children that they are going to play some different games using a beanbag:
  - ❖ **Game 1**

    Ask the children to balance a beanbag on their hand and walk from one side of the room to the other. Then ask whether they can balance a beanbag on their foot or their head and walk again. Encourage the children to think of any other places they might balance a beanbag, such as their elbow, their knee or their shoulder.
  - ❖ **Game 2**

    Support the children in throwing the beanbags to each other and trying to catch them.
  - ❖ **Game 3**

    Put up some skittles and ask the children to try to knock them down using the beanbags.
  - ❖ **Game 4**

    Place a bucket or a hoop a short distance from the children and ask them to try to throw the beanbags into it.
  - ❖ **Game 5**

    Set up an obstacle course and invite children to try to complete it while balancing beanbags on their heads.

Extensions

- ◆ Repeat the activities with balls instead of beanbags.
- ◆ Make a beanbag. Seal some dried beans in a plastic bag. Stitch a felt bag, put the plastic bag of beans inside it and stitch up the opening firmly.

Links to the Early Learning Goals

- ◆ Physical development: Moving and handling
- ◆ Communication and language: Listening and attention, Understanding
- ◆ Personal, social and emotional development: Making relationships
- ◆ Expressive arts and design: Being imaginative

Trolley dash

Resources
Toy trolleys or prams; chalk; cones; play grocery items

Group size
Small groups

Learning objectives
◆ Control and coordination in large movements, especially pushing and pulling
◆ Confidence in handling and balancing equipment
◆ Following instructions and routes in order to participate in group activities
◆ Interacting and cooperating with others

Activity
◆ Use chalk to mark out a route and place cones on the route as obstacles.
◆ Mark out at least four different routes with start and finish lines in different places.
◆ Place some play grocery items along various parts of each route.
◆ Give each child a toy trolley or pram.
◆ Explain to the children that they will need to push their trolley along the route, going carefully around the cones, picking up and placing the grocery items in the trolley and running to the finish line.
◆ Explain to the children that the aim is not to be first across the finish line but to stick as closely as possible to the route.
◆ Ensure that the children are ready at their starting lines and give them a signal to go.

Extensions
◆ Set different extra tasks along the routes. For example, ask children to put on coats or balance beanbags on their heads.
◆ Put extra weight into the trolleys and find out whether this makes them easier or harder to push.
◆ Make a trolley out of boxes and string and ask the children to pull it along.
◆ Offer free play with other wheeled toys, such as scooters, tricycles, bicycles and pull-along carts.

Links to the Early Learning Goals
◆ Physical development: Moving and handling
◆ Communication and language: Listening and attention, Understanding
◆ Personal, social and emotional development: Making relationships

Traffic light game

Resources
Large open space; stethoscope

Group size
Whole class

Activity
◆ Explain to the children the rules for the traffic light game: red means stop, amber means walk and green means run.
◆ Remind the children to take care and to be aware of everybody's movements, when they are running around, so that they do not bump into each other.
◆ Ask the children to listen to their heartbeats while they are sitting quietly. Show them how to do this with their fingers or use a stethoscope.
◆ Now play the game, encouraging the children to respond appropriately when they hear the different colour names called out.
◆ Stop the game and ask the children to try to listen to their heartbeats again.
◆ Talk with the children about the other changes in their bodies caused by playing the game, such as a faster pulse rate, sweating, red faces and noisier breathing.

Extensions
◆ Repeat the game using different words to mean 'stop', 'walk' and 'run', such as the names of fruits or vegetables.
◆ For example, suggest that blue could mean 'jump up and down' and purple could mean 'hop around'.
◆ Encourage the children to take turns to lead the game and call out the colour names.
◆ Play other cooperative group games that involve physical skills and movements, such as Musical statues and What's the Time Mr Wolf?

Links to the Early Learning Goals
◆ Physical development: Moving and handling, Health and self-care
◆ Communication and language: Listening and attention, Understanding
◆ Personal, social and emotional development: Making relationships

Play Activities for the Early Years
www.brilliantpublications.co.uk

Skittle fun

Resources

Empty plastic bottles with lids; sand; balls; paint; paint brushes; pen; chalk

Group size

Small groups

Learning objectives

◆ Control and balance in large and small movements
◆ Effective handling of equipment
◆ Counting skills
◆ Understanding and using vocabulary for addition and subtraction
◆ Following instructions and rules to participate in group games
◆ Cooperation and taking turns

Activity

◆ Explain to the children that they are going to make a skittles game.
◆ Ask the children to pour sand into 10 bottles, making them a third full and more stable, then put on the lids.
◆ Decorate the bottles and paint on numbers 1 to 10.
◆ Decide with the children how far apart the skittles should be and how far away the children should stand. Mark with chalk.
◆ Set the bottles in a triangular pattern.
◆ Now you are ready to play.
◆ Ask the children to stand behind the line and throw a ball to try to knock down as many skittles as they can.
◆ Ask children to count how many are knocked down and how many are left standing in each turn.
◆ Count how many the children knock down and give them an equivalent number of counters or stones after each turn. If they have two or more turns each, they can use the counters or stones to help them to find their total scores.

Extensions

◆ Instead of skittles and balls, the game could be played with kitchen roll tubes and bean bags.
◆ Do basic subtraction/addition using skittles. Count how many have been knocked down. Take away from 10 to find how many are left.
◆ Practise number bonds by working out how many skittles have been knocked down and how many are still standing.
◆ Record the results on a chart to make a pictoral record of the addition and the game scores.
◆ Score instead by adding together the numbers on the bottles knocked down in each turn.
◆ Play different games using the bottles and a ball.

Links to the Early Learning Goals

◆ Physical development: Moving and handling
◆ Communication and language: Understanding
◆ Personal, social and emotional development: Making relationships
◆ Mathematics: Numbers

Easy catch

Resources
Old oven mitts; felt; self-adhesive Velcro®; glue; tennis balls

Group size
Pairs

Learning objectives
◆ Control and balance in large movements
◆ Effective handling of equipment
◆ Spatial awareness and how distances affect skills and movements
◆ Counting skills
◆ Following instructions and rules to participate in group games
◆ Cooperation and taking turns

Activity
◆ Explain to the children that they could make a game called 'Easy catch'.
◆ Start by asking the children to stick Velcro® to the tennis balls.
◆ Now ask them to glue felt to the oven mitts.
◆ When the glue has had time to dry, the games can begin.
◆ Decide how far apart the children should stand and mark with chalk if necessary.
◆ One person can throw a ball and another can try to catch it, wearing an oven mitt.
◆ The Velcro® should stick to the mitt.
◆ Encourage children to take turns to throw and to catch and to play in pairs and groups.

Extensions
◆ Increase the distance between the catcher and thrower to make the game more difficult.
◆ Play catch using other items such as beanbags (see Beanbag games, page 48).
◆ Count how many times children can catch the ball before dropping it.

Links to the Early Learning Goals
◆ Physical development: Moving and handling
◆ Communication and language: Understanding
◆ Personal, social and emotional development: Making relationships
◆ Mathematics: Numbers

Musical cushions

Resources
Cushions; a source of music

Group size
Large groups

Learning objectives
◆ Control and balance in large movements
◆ Effective handling of equipment
◆ Spatial awareness and how distances affect movements
◆ Listening and concentration skills
◆ Following instructions and rules to participate in group games
◆ Counting, addition and subtraction skills

Activity
◆ Introduce the game of 'Musical cushions' to the children and explain its rules. Remind the children that they should dance and move around the room while the music plays and sit down on a cushion when it stops.
◆ Remind the children to take care and to be aware of everybody's movements, when they are dancing around the room, so that they do not bump into each other.
◆ Start by asking children to find a space. Show them how to check they have enough space by spreading their arms out wide and turning in a circle. If they touch anyone else they need to move.
◆ Play the game, removing one cushion after each turn. The winner is the last child left in the game. This is optional and it may be better not to remove cushions or ask children to sit out if the group is younger or less experienced, but simply to dance and stop together several times.

Extensions
◆ Play other variations of the game, such as Musical bumps, Musical statues, Musical chairs or Musical islands.
◆ Count how many cushions there are and ask the children how many will be left if one is removed.
◆ Play different types of music and ask the children to move accordingly (see Painting to music, page 193, and Move to the music, page 204).
◆ Use a musical instrument, played by an adult or a child, instead of recorded music.

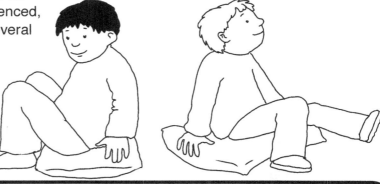

Links to the Early Learning Goals
◆ Physical development: Moving and handling
◆ Communication and language: Listening and attention, Understanding
◆ Personal, social and emotional development: Making relationships
◆ Mathematics: Numbers

Relaxation time

Resources
Soothing music

Group size
Whole class

Learning objectives
◆ Awareness and understanding of relaxation and its health benefits
◆ Awareness of names for various body parts
◆ Spatial awareness and control of small movements
◆ Observation of changes in the body when active or relaxed
◆ Listening and concentration skills

Activity
◆ Try to make this activity a regular feature of every day, either at the beginning or end of the day or before lunch.
◆ Explain to the children that they are going to have some relaxation time.
◆ Explain that the word 'relaxation' means to wind down and rest the mind and the body.
◆ Ask the children to lie on the floor and close their eyes. Ask them to make sure they have their own space and cannot touch anyone else.
◆ Stress the importance of keeping quiet and still.
◆ Play some soothing music.
◆ Explain that the word 'tensing' means squeezing and tightening.
◆ Ask the children to start by tensing their body and then relaxing it.
◆ Go through each part of the body, starting with the feet and ending with the face, tensing and relaxing.
◆ Finish by letting the children lie still and listen to the music for a minute or two.
◆ Ask the children to open their eyes and sit up slowly.
◆ Talk about how the children feel before and after the session. Discuss how their body feels when they are active and how it feels when they are resting.

Extensions
◆ Invite the children to compose their own relaxation music.
◆ Encourage children to take part in a creative activity, such as painting, before and after the relaxation session and find out whether it makes a difference to the way they approach the activity.
◆ Measure the difference in the children's heartbeat before and after relaxation time (see Traffic light game, page 50).

Links to the Early Learning Goals
◆ Physical development: Moving and handling, Health and self-care
◆ Communication and language: Listening and attention, Understanding

Is it healthy?

Resources

Healthy food: fruit, vegetables, brown bread, pure juices, eggs, cheese; unhealthy food: crisps, sweets, cakes, chips, fizzy drinks; large poster-size paper; scissors; glue; felt-tip pens

Group size

Whole class, then small groups

Learning objectives

◆ Listening and speaking skills
◆ Awareness and understanding of the importance of a healthy diet and which foods contribute to this.
◆ Fine motor skills
◆ Cooperation and interaction with others to participate in group activities

Activity

◆ Show the children different types of food and ask them which they think are healthy and which are unhealthy and why they think this.
◆ Talk about the terms 'healthy' and 'unhealthy' and discuss why it is important to eat healthy food.
◆ Encourage children to work together in small groups.
◆ Give each group two large sheets of paper and ask them to make two posters: one showing healthy food and one showing unhealthy food.
◆ Provide magazines so that they can cut out pictures. Encourage them to think about the layout of the poster.
◆ Invite children to share their posters and talk about them to the rest of the group.

Extensions

◆ Encourage children to use knives and other tools safely to help to prepare some healthy snacks, such as a fruit salad, to eat together.
◆ Talk about all the people who help keep us healthy, such as doctors, dentists, opticians and nurses.
◆ Show posters and adverts for healthy foods.
◆ Provide leaflets about healthy eating.
◆ Invite a dietician to come into the setting and talk with the children about healthy eating and a balanced diet.

Links to the Early Learning Goals

◆ Physical development: Moving and handling, Health and self-care
◆ Communication and language: Listening and attention, Understanding, Speaking

Healthy teeth

Resources

Healthy teeth sheet (see page 57); pieces of small white card; magazines; scissors; glue

Group size

Small groups

Learning objectives

- Awareness and understanding of the importance of healthy teeth
- Awareness and understanding of general good health and personal hygiene
- Meeting personal and hygiene needs independently
- Fine motor skills
- Listening and speaking skills

Activity

- Explain to the children that they are going to learn about teeth.
- Ask them to point to their teeth and even count them.
- Discuss with the children why they need teeth and why it is important that they look after them. Talk about how they can look after their teeth and which foods can be harmful to teeth.
- Give each group of children a photocopy of the Healthy teeth sheet.
- Ask them to stick on small pieces of white card for teeth.
- Now ask them to cut out pictures from magazines of food that will harm their teeth and stick these on the teeth.
- Give them another copy of the sheet and repeat the activity with pictures of food that is good for their teeth.
- Compare the two mouths and ask them what will happen to the teeth in each case.

Extensions

- Invite a dentist to come to talk to the children.
- Read *Freddie Visits the Dentist* by Nicola Smee (Barrons Educational Series).
- Give the children toothbrushes to clean their dolls' teeth.
- Put a tooth into a glass of cola and see what happens to it over a period of time.
- Talk about the correct way to brush teeth.
- Make a bar chart of favourite toothpastes.
- Look at the teeth of different animals.

Links to the Early Learning Goals

- Physical development: Moving and handling, Health and self-care
- Communication and language: Listening and attention, Understanding, Speaking

Healthy teeth sheet

Healthy food plate

Resources
Shopping bag containing healthy and unhealthy foods; lunch box containing healthy and unhealthy foods; paper plates; felt-tip pens

Group size
Whole class

Activity
◆ Show the children the shopping bag and ask them to sort the food into two piles: one healthy, the other unhealthy.
◆ Discuss why some foods are healthy and others are unhealthy. For example, milk is good as it contains calcium to keep bones strong; cola is unhealthy because it contains lots of sugars that cause tooth decay.
◆ Offer the lunchbox to the children and encourage them to sort the food into the two groups as before.
◆ Give each child a paper plate and on it ask them to draw healthy food that they would like to eat.
◆ Invite the children to share their plates with the group and to discuss why the foods they have drawn are healthy.

Learning objectives
◆ Listening and speaking skills
◆ Awareness and understanding of good health and a healthy diet
◆ Awareness of the ways that different foods affect different parts of the body
◆ Fine motor skills

Extensions
◆ Ask children to look into their lunchboxes and decide which foods are healthy or unhealthy.
◆ Stick pictures of healthy foods onto cards, laminate the cards and offer them to the children for use as place mats.
◆ Draw around a child to make a body shape. Stick on pictures to show the types of food needed to keep each part of the body healthy: for example, milk for teeth, fruit and vegetables for skin, meat for growth, etc.
◆ Make a healthy snack such as fruit kebabs (see Fruit kebabs, page 148).

Links to the Early Learning Goals
◆ Physical development: Moving and handling, Health and self-care
◆ Communication and language: Listening and attention, Speaking

Going on a Bear Hunt

Resources

Book: *We're Going on a Bear Hunt* by Michael Rosen (Walker Books); mats; apparatus (eg ropes, benches, ladders)

Group size

Whole class

Learning objectives

- Control and coordination in large movements.
- Challenge and imagination in role-play
- Concentration and understanding to recreate a story
- New vocabulary of words to describe positions and opposites

Activity

- Begin by reading the story *We're Going on a Bear Hunt*.
- Discuss the different ways that the characters tried to travel, such as over, under and through the obstacles on their route.
- Invite the children to act out the story while you read it again.
- Show the children the apparatus.
- Challenge the children to find as many different ways of travelling over, under, through and around the apparatus as possible.
- Invite children to demonstrate some of their favourite movements to the group.

Extensions

- Retell the story but change the animal featured in it. For example, there could be a tiger or a dragon in the cave.
- Tell the story from the point of view of the bear. For example, begin, 'I was fast asleep when suddenly ….'
- Count how many different ways the children find to travel across a piece of apparatus.
- Ask the children to suggest different areas that they could go to in the hunt and how they would travel over them. For example, they might scramble over a hill, or walk carefully across a road.

Links to the Early Learning Goals

- Physical development: Moving and handling
- Communication and language: Listening and attention, Speaking
- Expressive arts and design: Being imaginative

Grand Old Duke of York

Resources

Two wooden blocks with steps or sets of low steps

Group size

Large groups

Learning objectives

- Control and coordination in large movements
- Challenge and imagination in role-play
- Concentration and understanding to recreate a familiar song
- New vocabulary of words to describe positions and opposites
- Interacting and cooperating within a group and taking turns to lead

Activity

- Begin by singing the rhyme 'The Grand Old Duke of York'.
- Set up the steps back to back to form a hill.
- Invite children to act out the song.
- Model marching around the room and encourage the children to join in and march in a long line, taking turns to lead and to follow.
- Introduce the idea of marching up and down the hill, using the sets of steps, and support children in learning and practising this safely.
- Encourage children to sing the song while marching up and down appropriately.

Extensions

- Make costumes for the Duke and his soldiers.
- Decorate the steps, with the children, so that they look more like a hill.
- Count the number of children and change the song (eg 'The Grand old Duke of York, he had five men...').
- Count how many steps there are going up and how many coming down.
- Play 'Follow my leader' with the children, involving different activities, such as balancing along a bench, stepping through a hoop or crawling under a rope.

Links to the Early Learning Goals

- Physical development: Moving and handling
- Personal, social and emotional development: Making relationships
- Expressive arts and design: Exploring and using media and materials, Being imaginative

Clay pot

Resources

Clay; waxed paper; water; aprons; circular cutters; rolling pins; paint; paint brushes

Group size

Small groups

Learning objectives

◆ Fine motor skills
◆ Challenge and stimulation of exploring new materials and techniques
◆ Following instructions and examples in order to understand and participate in a new project
◆ Counting skills

Activity

◆ Show the children a picture or an example of a clay pot and invite them to try to make one of their own.
◆ Ask the children to put on aprons.
◆ Give each child a block of clay on a sheet of waxed paper.
◆ Work alongside the children, modelling rolling out the clay and cutting a circular base, then rolling pieces of clay into 'sausage' shapes.
◆ Demonstrate how to use water to stick layers together and to attach the sausage shapes to the base, layer by layer, using fingers to blend the clay together well so that it doesn't fall apart in the oven.
◆ Put the finished pots in the oven to bake.
◆ Paint the pots and display with a label explaining how they were made.

Extensions

◆ Make some other items from clay such as plates, name labels or pencil holders.
◆ Make pots using different materials.
◆ Compare clay when it is dry, wet and baked.
◆ Count the number of layers in each pot.

Links to the Early Learning Goals

◆ Physical development: Moving and handling
◆ Communication and language: Understanding
◆ Mathematics: Numbers
◆ Expressive arts and design: Exploring and using media and materials

Papier mâché ladybirds

Resources
Pictures of ladybirds; balloons; paste made from flour and water; newspaper torn into strips; plant pots; paint; paint brushes; pipe cleaners; sticky tape

Group size
Whole class working in pairs

Learning objectives
◆ Fine motor skills
◆ Challenge and stimulation of exploring new materials and techniques
◆ Following instructions and examples in order to understand and participate in a new project
◆ Interacting, cooperating and sharing with a partner to complete creative work
◆ Awareness and understanding of the features of a ladybird
◆ Counting skills

Activity
◆ Share pictures of ladybirds with the children and discuss their particular features, such as six legs, an oval body, wings and a symmetrical pattern of spots.
◆ Provide a blown-up balloon for each pair of children and help them to wedge them inside plant pots to keep them steady while they work on them.
◆ Show the children how to smear the balloon with the flour paste and then stick on newspaper strips. Support them as they repeat this until the balloons are covered in four layers of paper.
◆ Leave all the balloons to dry in a warm, dry place.
◆ When the balloons are dry cut them in half and give one half to each child.
◆ Give each child six pipe cleaners to attach as legs to their balloon half.

◆ Paint the ladybirds red or yellow and leave to dry.
◆ Paint a black central strip and spots onto the body.
◆ Display all the ladybirds on a background of giant paper leaves.

Extensions
◆ Read the poem 'Ladybird, Ladybird, Fly Away Home'.
◆ Write a story about a ladybird.
◆ Look for ladybirds in the outdoor area and find out where they live.
◆ Count the spots on ladybirds and compare them.
◆ Make an information book about ladybirds, explaining where they live and what they eat, etc.
◆ Read the story *The Bad-Tempered Ladybird* by Eric Carle (Puffin Books).

Links to the Early Learning Goals
◆ Physical development: Moving and handling
◆ Communication and language: Understanding
◆ Personal, social and emotional development: Making relationships
◆ Mathematics: Numbers
◆ Understanding the world: The world
◆ Expressive arts and design: Exploring and using media and materials

Personal, Social and Emotional Development

It is important that children develop a positive attitude to themselves and others in order to develop a high self-esteem and interact successfully with adults and peers. A feeling of self-worth, a willingness to socialize and an ability to control and manage emotions will be valuable to them throughout their lives.

The activities in this chapter help children to:
◆ develop a positive and confident attitude to learning and achievement
◆ verbalize their own feelings and empathise with others
◆ express feelings in language and through imaginative and creative play
◆ work independently or in large or small groups, taking turns and sharing
◆ understand rules, behavioural standards, moral values and consequences
◆ form positive relationships with adults and peers.

There are three Early Learning Goals (ELGs) within the prime area of Personal, Social and Emotional Development:

Self-confidence and self-awareness
Children are confident to try new activities, and say why they like some activities more than others. They are confident to speak in a familiar group, will talk about their ideas, and will choose the resources they need for their chosen activities. They say when they do or don't need help

Managing feelings and behaviour
Children talk about how they and others show feelings, talk about their own and others' behaviour, and its consequences, and know that some behaviour is unacceptable. They work as part of a group or class, and understand and follow the rules. They adjust their behaviour to different situations, and take changes of routine in their stride.

Making relationships
Children play cooperatively, taking turns with others. They take account of one another's ideas about how to organise their activity. They show sensitivity to others' needs and feelings, and form positive relationships with adults and other children.

The table on pages 64–65 shows which activities will help children to work towards, or achieve, these ELGs. Where an activity works towards ELGs in other areas, this has been indicated in the table.

Table of learning opportunities

Activity	Page no.	Communication and Language			Physical Development		Personal, Social and Emotional Development			Literacy		Mathematics		Understanding the World			Expressive Arts and Design	
		Listening and attention	Understanding	Speaking	Moving and handling	Health and self-care	Self-confidence and self-awareness	Managing feelings and behaviour	Making relationships	Reading	Writing	Numbers	Shape, space and measures	People and communities	The world	Technology	Exploring and using media and materials	Being imaginative
Happy/sad masks	66–68			✓				✓										
Find the hidden treasure	69			✓			✓					✓			✓		✓	
Guess the object	70										✓						✓	
My favourite toy	71	✓	✓	✓			✓	✓	✓					✓				
Feel and guess	72	✓	✓	✓			✓	✓	✓						✓			
Making puppets	73	✓					✓	✓	✓									✓
Sound game	74	✓					✓		✓									
Kim's game	75	✓					✓	✓	✓									
Praise cards	76								✓									✓
Happy family book	77							✓	✓					✓				
Golden rules	78			✓				✓	✓									
Crossing the road	79					✓		✓	✓									✓
Special clothes	80					✓			✓					✓				
Places of worship	81	✓		✓				✓	✓					✓				
Pen pal class	82			✓					✓		✓			✓		✓		

Play Activities for the Early Years
www.brilliantpublications.co.uk

Area	Aspect	Being new	Thank you cakes	Parachute play	The Boy Who Cried Wolf	What is wrong?	Nursery rhyme costumes	Spider perseverance	Sunflowers	Holiday times	Festivals	All about me
Expressive Arts and Design	Being imaginative	✓					✓	✓				
	Exploring and using media and materials		✓				✓					
Understanding the World	Technology											
	The world								✓	✓		
	People and communities									✓	✓	✓
Mathematics	Shape, space and measures											
	Numbers											
Literacy	Writing											
	Reading									✓		
Personal, Social and Emotional Development	Making relationships	✓	✓	✓	✓	✓	✓		✓	✓	✓	✓
	Managing feelings and behaviour	✓	✓	✓	✓	✓		✓	✓			
	Self-confidence and self-awareness					✓			✓		✓	
Physical Development	Health and self-care		✓				✓	✓				
	Moving and handling			✓					✓			
Communication and Language	Speaking	✓			✓	✓	✓	✓			✓	
	Understanding	✓	✓	✓	✓	✓	✓	✓				
	Listening and attention	✓		✓	✓	✓	✓	✓			✓	✓
Page no.		83	84–85	86–87	88	89–90	91	92–93	94	95	96	97

Happy/sad masks

Resources

Happy mask (see page 67); Sad mask (see page 68). Photocopy the masks onto card and glue sticks to back as handles.

Group size

Whole class

Activity

◆ Bring the children together as a group at the end of a session or school day.
◆ Ask the children to think, remember and reflect upon their feelings and experiences of the day.
◆ Show them the happy and sad masks.
◆ Invite each child in turn to choose the mask that demonstrates their feelings and to explain why.
◆ You can start by saying how you feel, for example: 'I chose the happy mask because I enjoyed playing in the role-play area with John and Sunita.'

Learning objectives

◆ Listening and speaking skills
◆ Expressing emotions in a safe and controlled manner
◆ Reflecting on past experiences

Extensions

◆ Make masks to represent other emotions: angry, excited, surprised, etc.
◆ Provide a variety of different resources and encourage children to make masks to their own designs.
◆ Show masks from other cultures, for example Chinese, African or Indian masks.
◆ Have a quiet area where children can go if they feel sad or angry.
◆ Discuss the things that make the children feel happy or sad and make a list together.

Links to the Early Learning Goals

◆ Personal, social and emotional development: Managing feelings and behaviour
◆ Communication and language: Speaking

Happy mask

Sad mask

Play Activities for the Early Years
www.brilliantpublications.co.uk

Find the hidden treasure

Resources

Sand tray full of sand; treasure (brightly coloured buttons, bead necklaces, shiny coins, plastic rings, etc); sieves; colanders; trays; paper; coloured pencils

Group size

Small groups

Learning objectives

◆ Confidence in trying new activities and choosing resources
◆ Curiosity, challenge and stimulation of exploring new materials and ideas
◆ Properties of sand
◆ Describing their activity through speech or drawing
◆ Counting, sorting and matching skills

Activity

◆ Hide the treasure in the sand tray.
◆ Invite the children to search for 'hidden treasure' in the sand tray.
◆ Show the children the different resources they can use to help them in their search (sieves, colanders, etc).
◆ When the children have found all of the treasure, they might like to draw pictures of what they have found.

Extensions

◆ Use water, sawdust or coloured rice instead of sand.
◆ Count the things the children found.
◆ Suggest to the children that they might like to make and hide some different treasure.
◆ Sort the treasure into hoops – by colour, size, etc.
◆ Extend the sand play by giving the children interesting sand equipment such as turning wheels, differently sized bottles, etc.
◆ Read *Spot's Treasure Hunt* by Eric Hill (Putnam Publishing Group).

Links to the Early Learning Goals

◆ Personal, social and emotional development: Self-confidence and self-awareness
◆ Communication and language: Speaking
◆ Mathematics: Numbers
◆ Understanding the world: The world
◆ Expressive arts and design: Exploring and using media and materials

Guess the object

Resources

An unusual object that children are not familiar with, such as an old clothes wringer or washboard

Group size

Large groups

Learning objectives

◆ Confidence in trying new activities and choosing resources
◆ Curiosity, challenge and stimulation of exploring new materials and ideas
◆ Describing objects through speech or writing

Activity

◆ Gather the children together in a circle.
◆ Show the children the unusual object and pass it round the circle for all the children to examine it in more detail.
◆ Ask the children to guess what it is.
◆ Encourage the children to ask questions.
◆ Tell the children the name of the object and explain its purpose.

Extensions

◆ Ask the children to bring in unusual objects from home.
◆ Set up a table with unusual objects and a note pad. Let the children explore them during free play and write on the note pad what they think they are.
◆ Provide resources, such as recycled and junk materials, and invite children to invent and create machines. Encourage them to guess what the machines might do.
◆ Under careful supervision, allow children to take apart some old objects, such as watches or clockwork toys. Be aware of any potential safety issues, such as very small parts or sharp pieces.

Link to the Early Learning Goals

◆ Personal, social and emotional development: Self-confidence and self-awareness
◆ Literacy: Writing
◆ Expressive arts and design: Exploring and using media and materials

My favourite toy

Resources
Children to bring in their favourite toy

Group size
Whole class

Learning objectives
- Approaching new activities and routines with confidence
- Interaction and cooperation with others and sensitivity to others' needs and feelings
- Taking turns and sharing within a group
- Understanding and following rules and adjusting behaviour for different situations
- Listening and speaking skills
- Expressing personal views and experiences confidently
- Awareness and understanding of similarities and differences between members of the group and their families and communities

Activity
- Invite the children to bring in their favourite toy (make sure they are labelled).
- Gather the children together into a circle.
- Introduce the idea of 'circle time', in which children can talk and listen to each other.
- Explain the two rules that make a circle time successful. Children must listen to each other and they may only speak when it is their turn.
- Make sure the children understand the importance and value of the rules.
- Invite the children to show and talk about their favourite toys in turn. Model attentive listening and not interrupting while each child talks and ensure that every child who wishes to has a turn to speak.
- Ask whether children would like to share their toys with friends and allow some free play time. Explain how important it is to take good care of other people's toys.
- Ensure that all toys are returned safely to their owners to be taken home.

Extensions
- Introduce a wide variety of topics at circle times.
- Make books of favourites with the children, such as favourite foods, favourite stories, favourite games, etc.
- Encourage children to make up stories about their own toys.
- Sort toys into hoops – by colour, shape, etc.
- Allow children to share other things at circle times, such as snacks, books or musical instruments.

Links to the Early Learning Goals
- Personal, social and emotional development: Self-confidence and self-awareness, Managing feelings and behaviour, Making relationships
- Communication and language: Listening and attention, Understanding, Speaking
- Understanding the world: People and communities

Feel and guess

Resources

A bag with a drawstring; different items for children to feel (eg soft teddy bear, wooden spoon, key, pine cone)

Group size

Small groups

Learning objectives

◆ Approaching new activities with confidence
◆ Taking turns and sharing within a group
◆ Understanding and following rules and adjusting behaviour for different situations
◆ Listening and speaking skills and new vocabulary
◆ Awareness and understanding of similarities and differences between objects and materials and their textures through the sense of touch

Activity

◆ Show the children the bag and invite them to take turns to feel the object inside and guess what it is.
◆ Encourage the children's descriptions and ideas by asking questions and inviting them to talk as much as they can about what they feel.
◆ Ask the children to wait until everyone has had their turn to feel and describe the object and then to say what they think it is.
◆ Reveal the object and let the children see whether their guesses were correct.
◆ Repeat the activity using other objects.

Extensions

◆ Adapt the game by blindfolding children and asking them to feel bowls of different items such as jelly, pasta, sawdust and rice.
◆ Make the game harder by giving objects which are similar to one another (eg the same shape – coins, buttons, washers, counters).
◆ Blindfold a child and ask them to feel another child's face and guess who it is.
◆ Place unusual objects into the bag.
◆ Instead of a feely bag make a feely box by taking a shoe box and putting a hole in the lid. Place an object inside. Let the children put their hand through the hole to feel.

Links to the Early Learning Goals

◆ Personal, social and emotional development: Self-confidence and self-awareness, Managing feelings and behaviour, Making relationships
◆ Communication and language: Understanding
◆ Understanding the world: The world

Making puppets

Resources
Pictures and books about puppets; socks; buttons; string; paper bags; wooden spoons; pieces of fabric; wool; glue; sticky tape; junk materials; scissors; paint; paint brushes

Group size
Small groups

Learning objectives
◆ Approaching new activities with confidence
◆ Creativity and imagination
◆ Group discussion and sharing of ideas
◆ Independent working skills with support
◆ Listening and speaking skills and new vocabulary

Activity
◆ Show the children books and pictures of different types of puppets.
◆ If possible take the children to see a puppet show or arrange for a puppet show to visit the setting.
◆ Encourage children to share ideas and discuss ways of making puppets with the available resources.
◆ Invite the children to make their own puppets. Encourage them to select their own resources and work independently, offering them support when it is needed or requested.
◆ Invite the children to show the finished puppets to each other and to explain to the group how they were made.

Extensions
◆ Use the puppets to make a puppet show (see Puppet theatre, page 27).
◆ Make up stories for the puppets to act out.
◆ Use puppets to discuss emotions.
◆ Retell stories using puppets.

Links to the Early Learning Goals
◆ Personal, social and emotional development: Self-confidence and self-awareness, Managing feelings and behaviour, Making relationships
◆ Communication and language: Listening and attention, Speaking
◆ Expressive arts and design: Being imaginative

Sound game

Resources
Different objects that make sounds (eg clocks, musical instruments, spoons, wind chimes, bells, etc)

Group size
Whole class

Learning objectives
◆ Listening and concentration skills
◆ Identifying familiar sounds and objects using only the sense of hearing
◆ Cooperation and turn taking within a group

Activity
◆ Gather the children and invite them to sit together as a group.
◆ Show the objects to the children and demonstrate the sounds they make.
◆ Encourage the children to sit quietly and concentrate.
◆ Invite children one by one to choose an object and make its sound while the others close or cover their eyes and try to guess what it is.
◆ Repeat the activity to allow all children to take turns to make the sounds if they wish to.

Extensions
◆ Clap a pattern and ask children to repeat it using one of the objects.
◆ Ask the children to use objects to make music.
◆ Make up a short poem about things that make a noise. For example:

> The clock goes tick, tock,
> The bell goes ting-a-ling.

◆ Read the story *Peace at Last* by Jill Murphy (Macmillan Children's Books).

Links to the Early Learning Goals
◆ Personal, social and emotional development: Self-confidence and self-awareness, Making relationships
◆ Communication and language: Listening and attention

Kim's game

Resources

Tray of different items (eg clock, pen, key, ball); cloth to cover tray; flip chart; pen

Group size

Large groups

Learning objectives

◆ Approaching new activities with confidence
◆ Improving attention, concentration and thinking skills
◆ Developing visual memory skills
◆ Cooperation within a group

Activity

◆ Introduce the children to 'Kim's game'. Explain how to play and encourage children to concentrate and use and develop their memories.
◆ Show the children the tray of objects covered by the cloth and explain that it will be uncovered for just a short period of time during which everybody must look carefully and try to remember all the objects.
◆ Remove the cloth for about a minute and then cover the tray again.
◆ Ask the children to tell you what was on the tray, and write their guesses on a flip chart.
◆ Uncover the tray and see if they were right.

Extensions

◆ Start with just three objects and then increase the number to make it harder.
◆ Make the game harder by asking children to remember not only the objects but also their position on the tray.
◆ Count how many items are on the tray.
◆ Use objects that look similar to make the game more challenging.

Links to the Early Learning Goals

◆ Personal, social and emotional development: Self-confidence and self-awareness, Managing feelings and behaviour, Making relationships
◆ Communication and language: Listening and attention

Praise cards

Resources

Small name card for each child; bag; card; felt-tip pens; glitter; sticky paper; fabric scraps; stars; glue

Group size

Whole class

Activity

◆ Place all the card names inside the bag and shake.
◆ Gather the children together and invite them to sit in a circle.
◆ Ask each child to pick a name from the bag.
◆ Taking turns around the circle, ask each child to say one thing that they like about the person whose name is on the card they picked.
◆ Invite each child to make a card for that person using the variety of resources available. Encourage them to work independently, offering support only where needed or requested.
◆ Bring children together again to give and receive their cards.

Learning objectives

◆ Listening and speaking skills
◆ Improved self-esteem through receiving praise from others
◆ Social skills

Extensions

◆ Ask the children to work together on other activities (eg reading a book together).
◆ Invite the children to share toys with each other (see My favourite toy, page 71).
◆ Share food at snack time (see International food, pages 183–184).
◆ Invite children to work in pairs and to find out as much information as possible in order to make a book about each other.

Links to the Early Learning Goals

◆ Personal, social and emotional development: Making relationships
◆ Communication and language: Listening and attention
◆ Expressive arts and design: Being imaginative

Happy family book

Resources

Empty workbooks (or sheets of blank paper stapled together to make books); crayons, pens, etc

Group size

Whole class, then small groups

Learning objectives

◆ Listening and speaking skills
◆ Understanding feelings and emotions and how to express them
◆ Understanding how others show their emotions and becoming sensitive to their needs and feelings
◆ Understanding similarities and differences between people and their families

Activity

◆ Begin by discussing the term 'happiness'. Ask the children to talk about what makes them happy.
◆ Give each child a workbook and ask them to draw a picture of themselves and what makes them happy on the first page.
◆ On the other pages ask them to draw other members of their family.
◆ Ask the children to take their books home and ask their family members to draw what makes them happy beside the pictures of themselves.
◆ When the books are returned to the setting, encourage children to discuss with each other the things that make different people happy and to listen carefully to others' ideas and findings.
◆ Display the books in the book corner for children to share.

Extensions

◆ Repeat the activity to explore a different emotion.
◆ Make happy and sad masks (see Happy/sad masks, pages 66–68).
◆ Make a book about feelings. Start each page: I am happy when… I am angry when… I am excited when…, etc.
◆ Sing the song 'If You're Happy and You Know It Clap Your Hands'.
◆ Match actions to emotions. For example, to express anger the children might frown and stamp their feet (see Feeling faces, pages 196-197).

Links to the Early Learning Goals

◆ Personal, social and emotional development: Managing feelings and behaviour, Making relationships
◆ Understanding the world: People and communities

Golden rules

Resources
Flip chart and felt-tip pens; golden pen

Group size
Whole class

Learning objectives
- Understanding needs and feelings and how to express them
- Becoming sensitive to the needs and feelings of others
- Understanding the concepts and importance of self-control and self-discipline
- Understanding the concept of rules and their purpose
- Listening and speaking skills

Activity
- Discuss with children the conditions they would like for playing and learning in their setting. Encourage them to talk about their needs and wishes and what they like or dislike.
- Explain what 'rules' are and invite the children to think of some rules that everybody must follow to keep themselves and others safe and happy.
- Encourage all children to express their views in turn and to listen carefully to each other and comment on what is said.
- Write down all the suggestions and support the children in choosing the five most important and relevant to the group.
- Write these 'golden rules' out clearly with a golden pen and explain that they must be adhered to by everybody in the group. Decide the consequences of a rule being broken and make sure that all children understand clearly and accept both the rules and the consequences as fair.
- Display the golden rules in a prominent place and remind children of them at intervals and appropriate times.

Extensions
- Talk about rules in different places and their purposes. For example, the rules of the road are to keep people safe and the rules at home are to make life fair for all family members.
- Reward children who remember and follow the rules with praise, extra privileges or favourite play activities.
- Before an outing, discuss safety and behavioural rules.
- Before inviting visitors into the setting, discuss with the children behavioural rules and how to be sensitive to the needs and feelings of the visitors.

Links to the Early Learning Goals
- Personal, social and emotional development: Managing feelings and behaviour, Making relationships
- Communication and language: Speaking

Crossing the road

Resources
A hard surface in the outdoor area marked out as a road (include zebra crossing and traffic lights); play cars, bicycles and tricycles

Group size
Large groups

Learning objectives
◆ Awareness and understanding of the road as a potentially dangerous place
◆ Understanding how to stay safe
◆ Understanding the needs of both pedestrians and drivers
◆ Practising road safety skills through role-play

Activity
◆ Talk to the children about how they cross roads. Discuss where is it safe to cross and why people need to take care?
◆ Remind the children of some basic road safety rules, such as always holding an adult's hand, standing on the pavement in a safe place and continuing to look and listen while crossing.
◆ Now talk to the children about the rules and needs of drivers. For example, they need to obey the speed limit, look out for pedestrians and stop at zebra crossings.
◆ Show the children the road area outside.
◆ Ask some children to be the pedestrians and some to be the drivers.
◆ Remind the pedestrians that they need to cross the road safely and the drivers that they need to drive carefully and look out for pedestrians.
◆ Play with the children and model appropriate behaviour, such as holding hands and crossing at the zebra crossing or pretending to drive a car and always stopping at the traffic lights.
◆ Encourage all children to take turns to be both drivers and pedestrians.

Extensions
◆ Invite a policeman to come into the setting and talk to the children about road safety.
◆ Talk to the children about staying safe in different circumstances, such as near to a river or a pond or out in a large shopping centre.
◆ Provide dressing-up outfits for police officers and lollipop attendants.
◆ Talk about the Green Cross Code and encourage children to remember it.

Links to the Early Learning Goals
◆ Personal, social and emotional development: Managing feelings and behaviour, Making relationships
◆ Physical development: Health and self-care
◆ Expressive arts and design: Being imaginative

Special clothes

Resources

Dressing-up clothes and hats from around the world: saris – India, salwar kameez – Pakistan, kimono – Japan, grass skirts – Hawaii; pictures and books of people in different national costumes

Group size

Whole class, then small groups

Activity

◆ Show pictures and books of people in different national costumes.

◆ Show the different items of dressing-up clothes and introduce the correct names.

◆ Encourage the children to touch the different items and to ask questions.

◆ Invite children to dress up in various outfits, using pictures as a guide to how to wear more unusual items, and supporting them as necessary.

◆ Encourage children to talk to the group about what they are wearing , which country the item of clothing comes from and its name. For example: 'I am wearing a sari from India.'

Learning objectives

◆ Recognizing and naming items of clothing from many countries of the world

◆ Dressing and undressing, independently or with support

◆ Awareness and understanding of other people's cultures and the need to respect them

Extensions

◆ Invite adults from different communities to show how to put on different clothing and help the children to dress up.

◆ Read the book *Children Just Like Me* by Barnabas and Anabel Kindersley (Dorling Kindersley Publishing).

◆ Ask the children to bring in some special clothing from home.

◆ Use different fabrics and patterns to make an international quilt.

◆ Ask if any staff or parents could make child-sized international clothing to be dressing-up outfits for the role-play area.

◆ Look closely at the patterns on saris. Try to copy them.

Links to the Early Learning Goals

◆ Personal, social and emotional development: Making relationships
◆ Physical development: Health and self-care
◆ Understanding the world: People and communities

Places of worship

Resources
Pictures, books, CD Roms or DVDs of different places of worship (church, mosque, synagogue, etc); camera; paper; pencils; clipboards; people from different communities

Group size
Whole class

Learning objectives
◆ Awareness and understanding of other people's cultures, beliefs and customs and the need to respect them
◆ Listening and speaking skills
◆ Observation skills

Activity
◆ Organize a trip to different places of worship (if possible try to cover most of the different religions of the children in the group).
◆ Show pictures and/or CD Roms or DVDs of the places before going.
◆ Prepare the children in advance for each visit, reminding them that they must respect other people's beliefs and customs (by covering their heads or removing their shoes, etc).
◆ During the trip take some photographs and, afterwards, encourage children to look at them and draw pictures of what they enjoyed.
◆ Invite some people from different communities to visit the setting and talk to the children.
◆ Prepare questions in advance and encourage the children to be respectful and listen attentively.
◆ Display the photographs and the children's pictures as a reminder of the trips.

Extensions
◆ Show artefacts from different places of worship.
◆ Make stained glass windows and other relevant artwork (see Stained glass windows, page 196).
◆ Talk about and celebrate different festivals: Hanukkah, Eid, Diwali, Holi.
◆ Make a journal telling the stories of the various visits.
◆ Show children scripts in various languages (see Books from around the world, page 116).
◆ Listen to religious songs in different languages.

Links to the Early Learning Goals
◆ Personal, social and emotional development: Managing feelings and behaviour, Making relationships
◆ Communication and language: Listening and attention, Speaking
◆ Understanding the world: People and communities

Pen pal class

Resources
Large sheet of paper; pen; envelope; stamp; books about country where pen pal class is based

Group size
Whole class

Learning objectives
◆ Forming positive and stimulating relationships with people in other countries
◆ Awareness and understanding of other people's countries and cultures
◆ Awareness and understanding of similarities and differences between children in different countries
◆ Listening and speaking skills
◆ Communication through letter writing and technology

Activity
◆ Make contact with a school, nursery or other early years setting abroad and choose a class or group to form a 'pen pal' relationship with.
◆ Talk to the class about the class abroad and read some books about the country they are in.
◆ Ask the children to decide what they would like to write to the class and scribe a letter on a large sheet of paper.
◆ Encourage children to provide information about themselves and also to think about specific questions they would like to have answered.
◆ Send the letter to the other class. If possible include some photos and pictures the children have made.
◆ The recipient class and teacher can then respond in a similar fashion.
◆ A relationship is now formed where both classes can learn about each other.

Extensions
◆ Do a teacher swap.
◆ Make a recording of the children speaking or singing to send to the pen pal class.
◆ Exchange e-mails between the groups, and, if possible, set up a Skype connection, so that the children can see and speak directly to each other.
◆ Make a reference book about the country.
◆ Make a class book with the children's pictures and information about themselves.

Links to Early Learning Goals
◆ Personal, social and emotional development: Making relationships
◆ Communication and language: Speaking
◆ Literacy: Writing
◆ Understanding the world: People and communities, Technology

Being new

Resources
Book: *Blue Horse and Tilly* by Helen Stephens (Scholastic)

Group size
Whole class, then in pairs

Learning objectives
◆ Understanding needs and feelings and how to express them
◆ Becoming sensitive to the needs and feelings of others
◆ Listening and speaking skills
◆ Confident and imaginative role-play
◆ Interaction and cooperation with others within the group
◆ Understanding and responding to stories

Activity
◆ Read the story *Blue Horse and Tilly*.
◆ Talk about the story and how Tilly felt shy when she moved to her new house.
◆ Ask whether any of the children have moved house and, if so, how they felt about it.
◆ Ask the children to think how they could welcome a new child into the group. For example, they might ask their name, introduce themselves and invite them to join in and play.
◆ Encourage children to take on the roles of newcomer and welcomer during role-play and to swap roles frequently.
◆ Initiate a group discussion about the different ideas that the children developed during their role-plays.

Extensions
◆ Use puppets to discuss feelings and different scenarios.
◆ Talk about different feelings (happiness, sadness, etc), and ask the children to relate the feelings to their own experiences.
◆ Read the story *Can't You Sleep, Little Bear?* by Martin Waddell (Walker Books) and ask children to think about times when they were scared.
◆ Use other storybooks to raise discussions about feelings.

Links to the Early Learning Goals
◆ Personal, social and emotional development: Managing feelings and behaviour, Making relationships
◆ Communication and language: Listening and attention, Understanding, Speaking
◆ Expressive arts and design: Being imaginative

Thank you cakes

Resources
Recipe, ingredients and equipment for 'thank you' cakes (see page 85).

Group size
Small groups

Learning objectives
- Appreciation of people who help us
- Understanding feelings and emotions and how to express them
- Listening and speaking skills
- Basic cookery skills and experimenting with ingredients and decorations
- Cooperation, sharing and taking turns
- Personal hygiene for health and safety

Activity
- Explain to the children that, as a group, they are going to make some 'thank you' cakes.
- Ask each child to think of someone they would like to give the cakes to and why. Offer suggestions (secretary, lollipop attendant, caretaker, etc).
- Talk about the importance of good hygiene when cooking and ask the children to wash their hands, put on an apron and tie back their hair. Let them do this as independently as possible.
- Make the cakes as shown on the recipe sheet.
- Provide an opportunity for the children to invite the person they have chosen into the setting and to present the cakes to them.
- Finish by letting the children present the cake to the person they want to say thank you to.
- Sit together as a group and share the cakes.

Extension
- Make thank you cards to go with the cakes.
- Do some more cooking: pizzas, salads.
- Design and make some packaging for the cakes.
- Count how many cakes are made.

Links to the Early Learning Goals
- Personal, social and emotional development: Managing feelings and behaviour, Making relationships
- Communication and language: Understanding
- Physical development: Health and self-care
- Expressive arts and design: Exploring and using media and materials

Recipe for thank you cakes

Ingredients

100 g (4 oz) flour

100 g (4 oz) softened butter

100 g (4 oz) sugar

2 small eggs

To decorate the cakes

icing

hundreds and thousands

Equipment

bowl

spoon

baking tray

oven

paper cake cases

Activity

✴ Preheat the oven to 180°C/350°F, gas mark 4.

✴ Start by showing the ingredients.

✴ Help the children to weigh them and put all the ingredients in a bowl.

✴ Now stir the mixture. Allow all the children to do this in turn.

✴ Place the paper cases on the baking tray and ask the children to take turns to pour the mixture into the cases.

✴ Place in the oven for 15–20 minutes.

✴ Once baked and cooled allow the children to decorate the cakes as they wish.

Parachute play

Resources

Parachute games sheet (see page 87); parachute; sponge balls; different coloured beanbags; three adults

Group size

Whole class

Learning objectives

- Working together and trusting each other as a group
- Listening and concentration skills
- Following and understanding instructions in order to particpate in group games
- Cooperation and taking turns
- Control and coordination in large movements

Activity

- Explain to the children that they are going to play some games using the parachute.
- Spread out the parachute on the floor.
- Ask the children to sit just beyond the edge of the parachute but not to touch it.
- Space the adults evenly between the children.
- Before playing explain to the children that they need to listen very carefully and work together for the games to work successfully.
- Ask the children to kneel and hold the parachute in their hands.
- Now ask them to stand up.
- Begin by asking the children to slowly raise the parachute up and down. Help them to get used to the idea of playing with it.
- Play some of the games on the Parachute games sheet.
- Whilst the children are playing, remind them to carry on listening carefully and working together.
- End the session with activity 5 or 6 from the Parachute games sheet

Extensions

- Ask the children to make up some games they can play with the parachute.
- Use the parachute for drama work and with songs.
- Use the parachute as a tent and have story time sitting on it (see Parachute games sheet).
- Ask the children to work together for other activities such as painting a picture, building a model.
- Invite the children to make some food to share at snack time.

Links to the Early Learning Goals

- Personal, social and emotional development: Managing feelings and behaviour, Making relationships
- Communication and language: Listening and attention, Understanding
- Physical development: Moving and handling

Parachute games

1. Ask the children to pretend that the parachute is water. Start by keeping the parachute still like calm water in a pond, then move the parachute to form ripples, now raise it up and down to form waves. Finish by shaking it fast like a storm.

2. Throw a sponge ball onto the parachute. Ask the children to move the ball around but try not to let it fall off.

3. Keep the ball on the parachute, and ask children to throw the ball up as high as they can.

4. Put a couple of balls on the parachute. Ask the children to shake and bounce the balls.

5. Ask the children to pull the parachute over their heads and sit on it – like a tent. This is a good way to have quiet time.

6. Ask some children to lie under the parachute whilst the rest of the class raises it up and down to create a relaxing breeze.

7. Play games where some children run under the parachute while the rest of the group supports it. You could place some different coloured beanbags under the parachute. Choose children to go under the parachute to get a particular beanbag: 'Sophie, can you get me a green beanbag.?'

8. Repeat 7 but add different equipment such as quoits. You can make it more difficult by asking children to bring out two items: 'Sunil, can you get me the red beanbag and the yellow quoit.?'

The Boy Who Cried Wolf

Resources
Book: *The Boy Who Cried Wolf*; flip chart and pens

Group size
Whole class

Learning objectives
◆ Listening and speaking skills
◆ Social and cooperation skills within a group
◆ Understanding the importance of telling the truth
◆ Retelling and adapting stories and relating them to life experiences

Activity
◆ Begin by reading the story *The Boy Who Cried Wolf*.
◆ Discuss the story with the children. Ask them why they think that nobody listened to the boy and why he should have told the truth.
◆ Discuss the term 'honesty' and what it means. Help the children relate it to their own lives.
◆ Retell the story together, but imagine that, this time, the boy tells the truth. Scribe the story on a flip chart.

Extension
◆ Play a true or false game.
◆ Teach other values: respect, self-control, courage, etc.
◆ Read other books with similar themes.
◆ Watch the film *Pinocchio* (Walt Disney).

Links to the Early Learning Goals
◆ Personal, social and emotional development: Managing feelings and behaviour, Making relationships
◆ Communication and language: Listening and attention, Understanding, Speaking

What is wrong?

Resources
What is wrong? picture sheet (see page 90)

Group size
Large groups

Learning objectives
◆ Understanding which types of actions and behaviours are right and which are wrong and the reasons for this
◆ Listening and speaking skills
◆ Social and cooperation skills within a group
◆ Understanding the possible consequences of doing something wrong

Activity
◆ Show the children the picture sheet.
◆ Look at picture 1. Ask the children what the child is doing and why it is wrong. (The child is throwing rubbish on the floor – this makes the area very untidy and unhealthy.)
◆ Ask how the child could correct his mistake (eg put the rubbish in the bin).
◆ Now look at and discuss the other pictures on the sheet.

Extensions
◆ Discuss each action in more depth and relate it to the children's lives by asking questions, such as 'How can we keep the outdoor area clean?' or 'How do we cross the road safely?'
◆ Think about and discuss other examples of actions that are wrong, such as not listening to others.
◆ Make a list of class rules (see Golden rules, page 78).
◆ Give stickers/certificates to reward very good behaviour and major achievements (see Good manners certificate, pages 29–30).
◆ Make up a story about someone who does something wrong. Ask the children to finish the story.

Links to the Early Learning Goals
◆ Personal, social and emotional development: Managing feelings and behaviour, Making relationships
◆ Communication and language: Understanding, Speaking

What is wrong? picture sheet

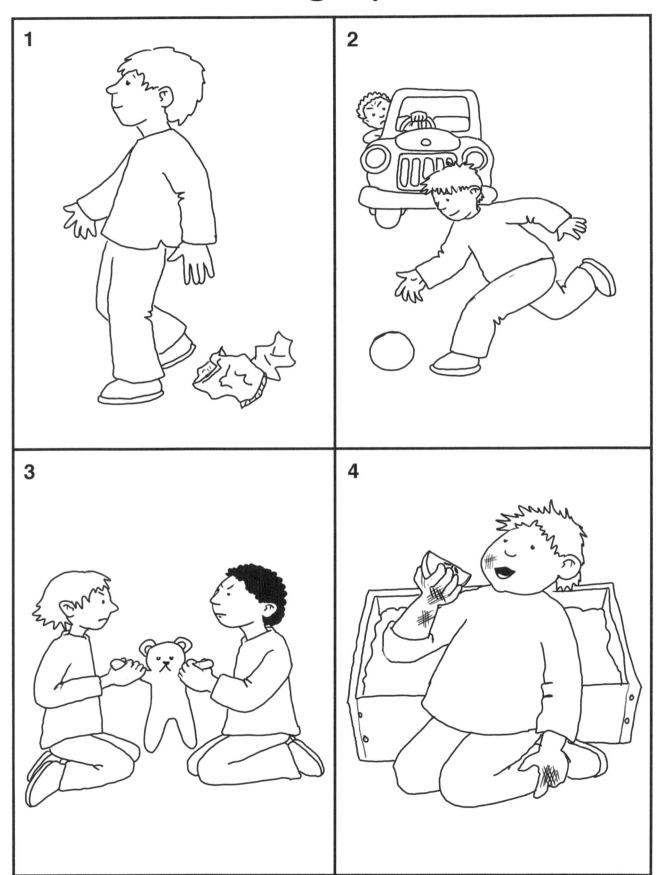

Play Activities for the Early Years
www.brilliantpublications.co.uk

Nursery rhyme costumes

Resources
A variety of dressing-up clothes and props; nursery rhyme books

Group size
Whole class, then small groups

Learning objectives
- Building up a repertoire of well-known nursery rhymes that can be confidently spoken or sung, individually or with the group
- Creative and imaginative role-play to recreate characters and events from rhymes
- Independent dressing and undressing skills

Activity
- Begin by reading some well-known nursery rhymes such as 'Humpty Dumpty' and 'Jack and Jill'.
- Show the children the dressing-up clothes.
- Divide the children into groups of two or three and give each group one nursery rhyme.
- Ask the children to play dressing up with the clothes and act out the nursery rhyme. Let them dress up independently.
- Invite groups to perform their rhymes to each other.

Extensions
- Perform the rhymes for staff, families or invited guests.
- Play an I spy rhyming game: 'I spy something that rhymes with "cat"' (see I spy rhyming game, page 14).
- Make some props in art work. For example, you could make a Humpty Dumpty by covering a balloon with papier mâché.
- Sequence pictures of nursery rhymes (see Nursery rhymes, pages 16–17).
- Encourage children to make up their own rhymes and record them.

Links to the Early Learning Goals
- Personal, social and emotional development: Self-confidence and self-awareness, Making relationships
- Communication and language: Listening and attention, Speaking
- Physical development: Health and self-care
- Expressive arts and design: Exploring and using media and materials, Being imaginative

Spider perseverance

Resources
Book: *The Very Busy Spider* by Eric Carle (Hamish Hamilton Children's Books); children's coats; The story of Robert the Bruce and the spider (see page 93)

Group size
Whole class

Learning objectives
◆ Listening and speaking skills
◆ Understanding the meaning and emotion of the word 'perseverance' and relating it to life experiences
◆ Independent dressing and undressing skills
◆ Taking pride in achievements

Activity
◆ Begin by reading the story *The Very Busy Spider*.
◆ Discuss the story and ask the children why they think the spider kept on working hard to finish his web.
◆ Talk about the legend of Robert the Bruce and the spider (see page 93).
◆ Introduce the word 'perseverance' and explain that it means to keep on trying to do something until it is achieved.
◆ Ask the children to think of situations in which they have persevered. For example, they may have tried to learn to tie their shoelaces, to ride a bike or to cut up their food by themselves.
◆ Ask them to think about how they felt when they had to keep on trying and how they felt when they accomplished the task.
◆ Encourage children to try to put on their own coats by themselves and to persevere if it is a hard task. (Some children will struggle to do this, but others will find it easy and will quickly need another challenge.)
◆ Emphasize that it is a hard task but they must persevere.
◆ Praise the children for their efforts.

Extensions
◆ Repeat the activity to encourage children to learn to tie their shoelaces or change their clothes.
◆ Talk about how sports stars have to practise over and over again.
◆ Make an achievement book where children can write down all the things they have mastered.
◆ Count the number of pieces of clothing that children take off and put on again if they change for a physical activity session.
◆ Provide an assortment of dressing-up outfits in the role-play area.
◆ Read the book *I Wish I Could Count to a Million* by Joyce Dunbar (Hodder and Stoughton Children's Division).

Link to the Early Learning Goals
◆ Personal, social and emotional development: Managing feelings and behaviour
◆ Communication and language: Listening and attention, Understanding, Speaking
◆ Physical development: Health and self-care
◆ Expressive arts and design: Being imaginative

The story of Robert the Bruce and the spider

Hundreds of years ago Scotland had a king and his name was Robert the Bruce. He was a brave and wise king, but he lived in dangerous times. The king of England wanted to take over Scotland and make it part of England. Many times the great army of England fought against Robert and his small army. Robert and his army fought hard but they were beaten down at each hurdle. Finally Robert and his men were forced to flee.

Robert ran into the wood and hid in a cave. He was tired and sad and wanted to give up the fight. Whilst lying there he noticed a spider weaving its web. He watched as the spider wove its web slowly and carefully, but every time the web was nearly finished a gust of wind would break it down. Each time this happened the spider would start again to weave its web and each time the web was almost finished it would be broken. 'You, too, know what it's like to fail,' thought Robert.

But the spider did not give up. On its tenth attempt the spider succeeded in completing its web. Robert let out a shout of joy! He now knew he could not give up and he gathered his men to fight one more great battle. This time Robert and his army won and the king of England and his army were forced back to their own country.

Robert never forgot the spider and how it inspired him to his victory.

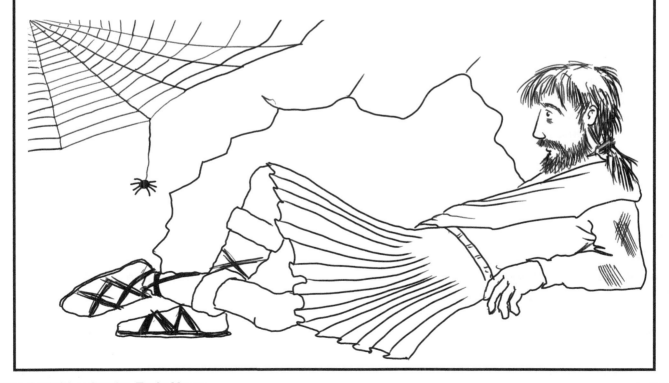

Play Activities for the Early Years
www.brilliantpublications.co.uk

93
This page may be photocopied by the purchasing institution only.

Sunflowers

Resources

Empty pots; soil; sunflower seeds; water; watering cans

Group size

Pairs

Learning objectives

- Cooperation, sharing and turn taking with a partner
- Caring for living things
- Taking some responsibility for remembering and carrying out regular tasks
- Fine motor skills
- Understanding the consequences of their actions or inactions
- Taking pride in achievements

Activity

- Explain to the children that they are going to plant some sunflower seeds to make the outdoor area look nice.
- Provide a pot for each pair of children. Ask them to put in some soil, place in the seeds and then cover with some more soil.
- Water the pots with the children and then explain to them that it is now their responsibility to water the pots regularly.
- Explain that the seeds will not survive without water, but that too much water is also bad.
- Encourage the children to decide which one of them is going to water and when.
- Point out that plants also need sunlight to grow so the children must decide on the best place to put their pots.
- Encourage the children to look after their plants independently.
- After two weeks check which plants have grown. If some have not grown, ask the children why.

Extensions

- Ask the children to plant some cress seeds in order to make sandwiches for lunch time – if they don't grow any, then they won't be able to make cress sandwiches.
- Invite the children to look after the class pet.
- Observe some mini-beasts. Ensure the children understand how to pick them up and handle them carefully.
- Talk about how the children look after any pets they have at home.
- Discuss the things plants need to grow (see My own garden, page 163).
- Read the book *Daisy's Giant Sunflower* by Emma Damon (Tango Books).

Links to the Early Learning Goals

- Personal, social and emotional development: Self-confidence and self-awareness, Managing feelings and behaviour, Making relationships
- Communication and language: Understanding
- Physical development: Moving and handling
- Understanding the world: The world

Holiday times

Resources
Map of the world; reference books about different countries

Group size
Whole class

Learning objectives
- Listening and speaking skills
- Awareness and understanding of names and locations of countries on a world map
- Gathering information about another country and its people, culture, climate, etc
- Cooperation, reading together, sharing books and information

Activity
- Begin by discussing holidays and the different countries the children have visited.
- Show the children a world map and discuss the colours. Explain that the blue indicates water and the green indicates land.
- Explain to the children that they are going to pretend that the whole class is going on holiday.
- Ask one child to point to a green area and read out the name of the country. This is the holiday destination.
- Ask the children what they already know about that country.
- Support children in looking at and reading books about the chosen country.
- Encourage the children to find out specific things such as what language is spoken there, what the weather is like, interesting places to see and different customs.
- Now discuss in a group the information the children found out.

Extensions
- Make a class book about the country.
- Have a country day. The children can dress in the traditional clothes of the country, listen to music, eat traditional food, etc.
- Cook a dish from the country, for example pizza from Italy, paella from Spain, chapattis from India (see International food, pages 183–184).
- Make a bar chart showing the number of children who have visited various countries.
- Set up chairs to resemble the inside of an aeroplane and support the children in role-play involving going on holiday.

Links to the Early Learning Goals
- Personal, social and emotional development: Making relationships
- Literacy: Reading
- Understanding the world: People and communities, The world

Festivals

Resources
No special requirements

Group size
Whole class

Learning objectives
◆ Awareness and understanding of a variety of festivals from different cultures
◆ Showing sensitivity to and respect for others' cultures, customs, beliefs and feelings and expecting this in return
◆ Listening and speaking skills
◆ Interaction and cooperation within the group to share information about festivals

Activity
◆ Talk to children about Christmas time and how it is a festival celebrated by Christians around the world.
◆ Ask the children if they celebrate any other festivals.
◆ Encourage the children to talk about the festivals they celebrate and encourage the rest of the group to ask questions such as: When is it celebrated? What special things do you do?
◆ Insist that the children listen carefully and show respect to the child who is speaking.
◆ Make a list of the festivals.
◆ Choose a festival to research further each term.

Extensions
◆ Invite people from other cultures to come in and speak to the children about the festivals they celebrate.
◆ Invite the children to bring in pictures or artefacts related to their festivals.
◆ Have a festival party.
◆ Learn different festival greetings. For example, to wish someone a happy Eid, one says 'Eid Mubarak'.
◆ Learn how to say hello and goodbye in different languages.
◆ Show children some dual-language books.
◆ Read *The Festival* by Peter Bonnici (Carolrhada Books) and *Samira's Eid* by Nasreen Aktar (Mantra Publishing).

Links to the Early Learning Goals
◆ Personal, social and emotional development: Making relationships
◆ Communication and language: Listening and attention
◆ Understanding the world: People and communities

All about me

Resources
Microphone

Group size
Whole class

Activity
◆ Gather the children together and invite them to sit in a circle.
◆ Show the children the microphone and explain that the children can only talk while they are holding it.
◆ Begin the activity by introducing yourself and saying a few words about yourself. For example, 'I am Mrs Patel, I am 30 years old, I am Indian, my favourite colour is yellow.'
◆ Now pass on the microphone to the child sitting beside you and invite him or her to say their name and a few words about themselves (how old they are, who is in their family, which religion they are, etc).
◆ Explain that when one child is speaking the other children must treat them with respect and listen carefully.
◆ Allow everybody to have a turn. Finish the activity by asking some questions to see if they have been listening carefully, such as which was a particular child's favourite colour.

Extensions
◆ Invite the children to make a book about themselves.
◆ Introduce discussions on other themes during circle times.
◆ Ask the children to work with their best friend and then make a book about them.
◆ Make a class year book with one page for each child. Include a photograph of the child and help them write a small autobiography.
◆ Ask the children to record a little about themselves.
◆ Read *All About Me* (Dorling Kindersley Publishing).

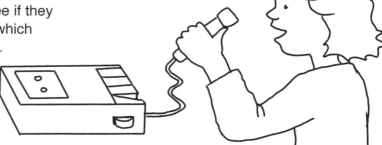

Links to the Early Learning Goals
◆ Personal, social and emotional development: Self-confidence and self-awareness, Making relationships
◆ Communication and language: Listening and attention, Speaking
◆ Understanding the world: People and communities

Literacy

The ability to understand language through reading and writing is a vital life skill that affects most areas of children's development as they grow older.

Children must be encouraged and supported to use and enjoy a wide variety of both fiction and non-fiction books, to explore and discover words and sounds and to write their own words and sentences, both for a purpose and for pleasure.

The activities in this chapter help children to:
◆ learn about the shapes and sounds of words
◆ appreciate stories, rhymes and information from books
◆ understand written language and begin to read independently
◆ experiment with letters and sounds and begin to write phonetically.

There are two Early Learning Goals (ELGs) within the specific area of Literacy:

Reading

Children read and understand simple sentences. They use phonic knowledge to decode regular words and read them aloud accurately. They also read some common irregular words. They demonstrate understanding when talking with others about what they have read.

Writing

Children use their phonic knowledge to write words in ways which match their spoken sounds. They also write some irregular common words. They write simple sentences which can be read by themselves and others. Some words are spelt correctly and others are phonetically plausible.

The table on pages 99–100 shows which activities will help children to work towards, or achieve, these ELGs. Where an activity works towards ELGs in other areas, this has been indicated in the table.

Table of learning opportunities

Activity	Page no.	Listening and attention	Understanding	Speaking	Moving and handling	Health and self-care	Self-confidence and self-awareness	Managing feelings and behaviour	Making relationships	Reading	Writing	Numbers	Shape, space and measures	People and communities	The world	Technology	Exploring and using media and materials	Being imaginative
		Communication and Language			**Physical Development**		**Personal, Social and Emotional Development**			**Literacy**		**Mathematics**		**Understanding the World**			**Expressive Arts and Design**	
Spider poem	101	✓			✓						✓							
Favourite animals	102			✓	✓					✓	✓							
Finish the sentence	103	✓	✓		✓					✓	✓							
Object game	104						✓			✓								
Same sound	105				✓					✓	✓							
Snap	106–107									✓						✓		
Alphabet biscuits	108–109				✓					✓	✓							
Letter of the week	110				✓						✓	✓						

Area	Aspect	Word lotto (111–112)	Word search (113)	Mixed-up sentence (114)	Making a book (115)	Books from around the world (116)	Shopping at the supermarket (117–118)	Mother's/Father's Day card (119–121)	Name t-shirt (122)	Three-letter words (123–124)
Expressive Arts and Design	Being imaginative						✓	✓		
	Exploring and using media and materials							✓	✓	
Understanding the World	Technology									
	The world									
	People and communities					✓		✓		
Mathematics	Shape, space and measures									
	Numbers		✓							
Literacy	Writing			✓	✓	✓	✓	✓	✓	✓
	Reading	✓	✓	✓	✓	✓	✓	✓		✓
Personal, Social and Emotional Development	Making relationships						✓			
	Managing feelings and behaviour									
	Self-confidence and self-awareness	✓			✓					
Physical Development	Health and self-care									
	Moving and handling		✓					✓	✓	✓
Communication and Language	Speaking									
	Understanding									
	Listening and attention									

Play Activities for the Early Years
www.brilliantpublications.co.uk

Spider poem

Resources
Poems and nursery rhymes about mini-beasts (eg 'Incy Wincy Spider'); flip chart and pens; large piece of paper

Group size
Whole class

Learning objectives
◆ Group work and cooperation
◆ Listening and speaking skills
◆ New vocabulary and understanding of poetry

Activity
◆ Share poems, rhymes and songs about mini-beasts, such as 'Incy Wincy Spider' with the children and introduce the idea of creating a new poem together.
◆ Explain to children that you are all going to work together and make up a poem about a spider.
◆ Write the word 'spider' down the side of the page:

> s
> p
> i
> d
> e
> r

◆ Explain that each line will start with each letter. In other words, the first line will begin with 's', the second with 'p' and so on. This type of poem is called an acrostic poem.
◆ Ask for suggestions of words that begin with each letter sound in turn and work with the children to bring all the ideas together to create a poem.
◆ Write out the poem on a large piece of paper shaped as a spider. Older or more able children could help with this. Encourage all children to write or mark make on spider shaped papers at their own levels.
◆ Display for all to enjoy.

Extensions
◆ Write a poem about another mini-beast in the same fashion.
◆ Write a rhyme about spiders, for example:

> Spiders are small
> They like to crawl
> They eat bugs and
> Like to hide in rugs.

◆ Listen to a wide range of stories, songs and poems about spiders and other mini-beasts.
◆ Use non-fiction books to find information about spiders.
◆ Make a spider out of junk material.

Links to the Early Learning Goals
◆ Literacy: Writing
◆ Communication and language: Listening and attention
◆ Physical development: Moving and handling

Favourite animals

Resources
Non-fiction books about animals; paper; pens and pencils

Group size
Pairs

Learning objectives
- Collaboration and cooperation skills
- Recognizing non-fiction books as sources of information
- Understanding the key features of non-fiction books
- New vocabulary and facts about books and animals

Activity
- Begin by discussing the difference between non-fiction and fiction books.
- Explain that the purpose of a non-fiction book is to provide information.
- Go through the features of a non-fiction book: contents page, index, etc.
- Ask children what their favourite animal is and why.
- Where possible, pair younger or less confident children with older or more able partners.
- Ask them to work together to find out some information about their animal using the non-fiction books provided. They could read and/or write some words or sentences or draw pictures about what interests them, depending on their ability and confidence levels.
- Invite each pair to talk to the rest of the group, or to an adult, about the information they gathered.
- Ask the children if they found out something that they did not know before.

Extensions
- The children could make reference books about their favourite animal. They may need an older child or adult to help them.
- Make a book about favourites, for example: 'My favourite colour', 'My favourite food'.
- When reading a non-fiction book ask the children to find the contents page and index.
- Ask the children to find books about other topics being studied.

Links to the Early Learning Goals
- Literacy: Reading, Writing
- Communication and language: Speaking
- Physical development: Moving and handling

Finish the sentence

Resources

Flip chart and pens; bag of descriptive words written on card (eg 'big', 'small', 'fierce', 'happy'); exercise books; pencils

Group size

Large groups

Learning objectives

- New vocabulary, particularly adjectives
- Understanding of the structure of a sentence and the need for punctuation
- Reading and writing simple sentences with support

Activity

- Write the start of a simple sentence on the flip chart and read it together. For example, 'The dog is _____'. Leave the end of the sentence blank.
- Ask one child to pick a word from a bag of descriptive words.
- Now write in the word to finish the sentence and read it together: 'The dog is fierce.'
- Talk to them about putting a full stop at the end to finish the sentence.
- Now do it again but choose a different ending.
- Older children could copy the sentence from the flip chart into their exercise books and then finish it with a word from the bag.
- Invite some of the children to try to read the sentences they have written.

Extensions

- Use some nonsense endings, for example, 'The dog is blue.'
- Ask children to come up with some other descriptive words.
- Display an outline picture of a dog and ask the children to fasten the sentences on to it with Blu-tack®.
- Cut up the words in a sentence and ask the children to place them in order to form the sentence again.
- Invite the children to use the cut-up words they know to form other simple sentences.

Links to Early Learning Goals

- Literacy: Reading, Writing
- Communication and language: Listening and attention
- Physical development: Moving and handling

Object game

Resources
Various objects from around the setting and brought in from home; pack of cards with letters of the alphabet on them

Group size
Large groups

Learning objectives
◆ Understanding and matching letter names and sounds
◆ Discovering initial and ending sounds in words

Activity
◆ Invite children to form a group and sit beside a pile of objects and a pile of alphabet cards.
◆ Ask one child at a time to pick a card and say the letter name and sound. For younger children limit the number of cards.
◆ Now ask them, to pick an object beginning with that letter from the objects in the middle.
◆ Ensure that every child who wants to can take a turn.

Extensions
◆ Ask the children to pick a child's name that begins with the letter they have picked.
◆ Ask the children to pick the object first and then say the letter sound.
◆ Record letter sounds so children can listen to and practise the sounds themselves.
◆ Cut out some pictures and ask children to write the letter sound of the object on the reverse.
◆ Write a sentence and ask children to circle how many of a certain letter sound they can see in it. Does the sound appear at the beginning, in the middle or at the end of each word?
◆ Play the game again, but this time ask the children to choose an object ending with the sound of the letter they have chosen.

Links to the Early Learning Goals
◆ Literacy: Reading
◆ Personal, social and emotional development: Self-confidence and self-awareness

Same sound

Resources
Paper; pencil; magazines; scissors; glue

Group size
Small groups

Learning objectives
◆ Understanding and matching letter names and sounds
◆ Discovering initial and ending sounds in words
◆ Writing names, independently or with support
◆ Fine motor skills

Activity
◆ Ask children to write their names on sheets of paper. You may need to scribe for some children.
◆ Support each child in identifying the letter sound at the beginning of their name.
◆ Now give the children magazines and ask them to find pictures of things beginning with the same sounds as at the beginning of their names.
◆ Ask the children to cut out the pictures they find and stick them onto the sheet of paper.
◆ Support some children in also identifying the sounds at the ends of their names and finding pictures of things that have those sounds, either at the end or at the beginning.

Extensions
◆ Break down the children's names into separate letters and ask the children to draw a picture to go with each letter. For example, for 'Tom' the child could draw a tomato, an orange and some milk.
◆ Play I spy.
◆ Record letter sounds which children can listen to in the listening area.
◆ Link actions to letter sounds so children can say and remember them. For example, for the letter 's' the children could do the actions of a snake whilst saying the sound. There are a number of phonic reading schemes which suggest actions, for example Jolly Phonics.
◆ Write the children's names with some letters missing, for example E_ily. Ask the children to work out the missing letter.

Links to the Early Learning Goals
◆ Literacy: Writing
◆ Physical development: Moving and handling

Snap

Resources

Snap cards (see page 107). (Photocopy onto card and cut up to produce two sets of cards.)

Group size

Pairs

Activity

- Ask children to work in pairs, to play Snap.
- Give each child a set of cards.
- Each player takes it in turn to put down a card. If the pictures on the cards start with the same letter sound (eg 'bed' and 'banana'), then the children need to call out 'Snap'.
- Continue playing until one player is out and the other player has all the cards.
- Now play a matching game.
- Spread out the cards on the table, face down.
- Ask each child to turn over one card and try to find another card with the same letters or sounds as their own names.
- Continue playing until all the cards are matched. The winner is the player with the most cards.

Learning objectives

- Understanding and matching letter names and sounds
- Discovering initial sounds in words
- Sorting and matching skills
- Letter recognition and word knowledge

Extensions

- Record letter names and sounds for the listening area. For example, 'The letter 'A' makes an 'a' sound,' (try to say just the letter sound and avoid saying 'uh' after the sound).
- Ask children to say the initial letter sounds in their names and the names of their friends.
- Ask children to think of things that begin with the same letters or sounds as their own names (see Same sound, page 105).
- Explore a different letter sound each week (see Letter of the week, page 110).
- Play with software packages on the computer which look at letters and letter sounds.

Links to the Early Learning Goals

- Literacy: Reading
- Understanding the world: Technology

Snap cards

Alphabet biscuits

Resources

Alphabet biscuits recipe and ingredients (see page 109); aprons; plastic knives or alphabet cutters

Group size

Small groups

Learning objectives

◆ Letter names, sounds, shapes and formation
◆ The ability to learn through touch and tactile experiences
◆ Using phonic knowledge to form words from sounds

Activity

◆ Start by asking the children to wash their hands and put on aprons.
◆ Read the recipe together and make up the biscuit mixture. Roll out the dough.
◆ Ask the children to use alphabet cutters or plastic knives to cut out some letters from the dough. Talk about the shapes of the letters.
◆ Ask the children to use the letters to make a simple word.
◆ Remind them to think of letter sounds when forming the words.
◆ Bake the biscuits and let them cool.
◆ Encourage the children to feel the shape of the letters.
◆ Finish by letting the children eat their words.

Extension

◆ Bake cakes and use icing to write words on top.
◆ Ask the children to write their names using biscuit letters.
◆ Make letters out of different materials: playdough, paper, clay, etc.
◆ Encourage the children to play games with wooden and plastic letters. For example, ask the children to put the letters in alphabetical order.
◆ Use letter stencils to write their names and other simple words.

Links to the Early Learning Goals

◆ Literacy: Reading, Writing
◆ Communication and language: Understanding
◆ Physical development: Moving and handling

Alphabet biscuits recipe

Resources

100 g (4 oz) of butter

50 g (2 oz) of sugar

150 g (6 oz) of flour

bowl

wooden spoon

sieve

rolling pin

baking tray

Activity

1. Preheat the oven to 150°C/ 300°F/ gas mark 2.

2. Beat the butter and sugar together.

3. Sieve the flour.

4. Add the flour to the butter and sugar mixture.

5. Use hands to form a dough.

6. Roll out the dough.

7. Make letter shapes using alphabet cutters or a plastic knife.

8. Place the biscuits on a greased baking tray and put in the oven for 20 minutes.

Letter of the week

Resources

Objects beginning with the letter of the week; paper; magazines; scissors; glue; pencils

Group size

Whole class

Learning objectives

- Understanding and remembering letter names and sounds
- Writing letters, independently or with support

Activity

- Choose the letter of the week and offer a variety of activities that can help to reinforce the letter's sound and formation.
- Show children how to write the letter and talk about the sound it makes.
- Bring in some objects beginning with the letter. Show them to the children and put on a display table.
- Give each child a sheet of paper and some magazines. Ask them to cut out and stick some pictures of things beginning with the letter of the week.
- Ask children to practise writing the letter. Ensure that they hold pencils correctly and form the letter correctly.
- Finish by playing an I spy game using only the letter of the week.

Extensions

- Make a class scrap book of letters. Use collage materials to form letters and draw pictures of things beginning with each letter.
- Choose a letter sound or even word of the week.
- Make things in art that begin with the letter, for example: a spiral card snake for 's', a puppet for 'p', a butterfly picture for 'b'.
- Give each child a page from a magazine. Ask them to circle the letter of the week on the page and to count how many times it appears.
- Make a list of words that the children can think of beginning with the letter and count them.

Links to the Early Learning Goals

- Literacy: Writing
- Physical development: Moving and handling
- Mathematics: Numbers

Word lotto

Resources

Word lotto cards (see page 112); counters. (Photocopy the sheet twice onto card. Cut one sheet along the thick lines to make four boards. Cut the other sheet to make 24 individual word cards.)

Group size

Small groups

Learning objectives
◆ Reading of simple, common words, using recognition and memory or phonics
◆ Matching of words, letters and sounds

Activity

◆ Give each child a lotto board.
◆ Place a stack of word cards in the middle of the table.
◆ Invite the children to pick a card in turn.
◆ Help them to try to read the word.
◆ Ask them to try to match the word to one of the words on their sheet.
◆ If the child has that word on their sheet they put a counter on it.
◆ Now it is the next child's turn.
◆ Carry on until someone wins by covering all of the words on their sheet with counters.

Extensions

◆ Make two sets of word cards and play Snap.
◆ Use cards to play matching and sorting games.
◆ Use the words to make simple sentences. Encourage children to try to sound out any words they are unsure of.
◆ Ask children to try to read the words independently.

Links to the Early Learning Goals

◆ Literacy: Reading
◆ Personal, social and emotional development: Self-confidence and self-awareness

Word lotto cards

are	the	he	no
I	go	Dad	cat
Mum	it	a	in
yes	play	dog	me
is	to	on	see
am	for	look	up

Play Activities for the Early Years
www.brilliantpublications.co.uk

Word search

Resources
Newspaper page – enlarged; common words (that the children have been learning) written on card (you could use page 112); pens

Group size
Large groups

Activity
- Begin by going through the word cards. Read the words together.
- Now give each child one word card and an enlarged copy of a newspaper page.
- Ask each child to find their word as many times as they can on the newspaper page and to circle it each time.
- Finish by asking the children to count how many words they found.
- See who found the most words and who found the fewest.

Learning objectives
- Understanding the concept of a word
- Understanding that print carries meaning
- Recognizing and reading simple and common words
- Developing visual discrimination
- Concentration skills

Extensions
- Repeat the activity, looking for a letter rather than a word.
- Make cards of other common words. Use them to play various games, such as Snap.
- Display common words so they are available for children to refer to every day.
- Whilst reading a book ask children to read the words they know.
- Write two sentences that are identical except for one word. Ask the children to spot the difference.

Links to the Early Learning Goals
- Literacy: Reading
- Mathematics: Numbers

Mixed-up sentence

Resources
Strips of paper; pencils; scissors; glue; workbooks (or paper)

Group size
Small groups, then individually

Learning objectives
◆ Recognizing and reading simple and common words
◆ Putting together words to form a sentence
◆ Writing simple words, using correct letter formation
◆ Holding and using a pencil effectively in order to write

Activity
◆ Ask a child to give you a sentence about what they like to do while at the setting. For example, 'I like to play football.'
◆ Write the sentence on a strip of paper.
◆ Now ask the child to read it with you.
◆ Cut up the sentence into separate words.
◆ Ask the child to put the words back into the correct order to make a sentence again.
◆ Let the children stick the words into their workbooks (or on a sheet of paper). Older children could be asked to write the sentence themselves underneath.
◆ Point out to the children the use of a capital letter at the beginning and a full stop at the end. Encourage them to use punctuation in their writing.

Extensions
◆ Write a sentence but miss off the ending. Ask children to add different endings (see Finish the sentence, page 103).
◆ Ask the children to count how many words they can read.
◆ Write the children's names and then cut up the letters and use them to make other words.
◆ Ask children whether they can read any of their friends' names.
◆ Ask older children to write their names on a board when they arrive at the setting, beside the activity they would like to choose. Younger children could stick their name card beside their chosen activity.

Links to the Early Learning Goals
◆ Literacy: Reading, Writing
◆ Physical development: Moving and handling

Play Activities for the Early Years
www.brilliantpublications.co.uk

Making a book

Resources
Photos of each child in the class participating in a variety of activities; hole punch; ribbon; pencil; pieces of card

Group size
Small groups

Learning objectives
◆ Recognizing the key features of a book
◆ Understanding that books provide information
◆ Listening and speaking skills
◆ Recognizing and writing names and simple, common words
◆ Building self-esteem and feeling positive about themselves

Activity
◆ As a group look at books and discuss the key features such as cover, words, pictures and author.
◆ Explain to the children that they are each going to make a book about themselves.
◆ Look and talk about the children's photos together.
◆ Ask each child to choose five photos for their book.
◆ Stick each photo onto a piece of card.
◆ Ask the child what they would like you to write for each picture and scribe for them.
◆ On each card write a simple sentence, always using the child's name first. For example, 'John is sleeping,' or 'John is eating.'
◆ Make a cover for the book.
◆ Hole punch each card.
◆ Use a ribbon to bind the pieces of card together.
◆ Finish the activity by reading the books together and then display them in a prominent place.

Extensions
◆ Ask more able children to form the sentences themselves using words they already know. Encourage them to sound out more complex words and attempt to write them themselves.
◆ Cut up the sentences and ask children to put in the correct order.
◆ Make the book using different materials. For example, you could make a zig-zag book by folding a long sheet of paper.
◆ Talk about fiction and non-fiction books and the differences. (See Book about me, page 37.)
◆ Work as a class and make up a story which can be made into a large book for shared reading.

Links to the Early Learning Goals
◆ Literacy: Reading, Writing
◆ Personal, social and emotional development: Self-confidence and self-awareness

Books from around the world

Resources

Books from different cultures (eg Arabic books – books read from 'back' to 'front' and lines from right to left, Chinese books – print is read top to bottom and from right to left, English books – read from top to bottom and left to right)

Learning objectives

◆ Recognizing the key features of a book
◆ Exploring similarities and differences between books from various cultures
◆ Comparing different scripts and alphabets
◆ Appreciating diversity

Group size

Large groups

Activity

◆ Talk to the children about the books in the classroom. Talk about how they hold the book and how they read and look at the pictures.
◆ Introduce and explain words such as 'title', 'author', 'illustrator'.
◆ Show how the book is read from top to bottom and left to right. Read a page using your finger to show where you are reading from.
◆ Now show them books from different cultures.
◆ Invite the children to look at how different languages are written.
◆ Talk about how the books are read. For example, explain that the front of an Arabic book is where we have the back, and that the back is where we have the front.
◆ Draw children's attention to different scripts and alphabets.
◆ Finish by displaying the books in the reading corner for the children to explore themselves.

Extensions

◆ Invite people from different communities to visit the setting and show how they read the books.
◆ Ask the children to attempt to write in different languages.
◆ Show the children alphabets in different languages. Count how many letters are in each.
◆ Ask the children to try to make an Arabic book – front on the right, back on the left.
◆ Invite the children to make their own picture storybook. Show them where to write their name as author/illustrator.
◆ Whilst reading books ask children to point to the title, author and illustrator.
◆ Children might be interested in looking for and discussing some authors' dedications in books.

Link to the Early Learning Goals

◆ Literacy: Reading, Writing
◆ Understanding the world: People and communities

Shopping at the supermarket

Resources

Supermarket role-play area with labels (see pages 118 and 169), till, grocery items (play food or real food, toy packets, tins and bottles or real ones that have been emptied and cleaned), baskets and play shopping trolleys

Group size

Small groups

Learning objectives

◆ Recognizing visual clues and that print carries meaning
◆ Understanding the purposes of reading and writing lists
◆ Creativity, imagination and making connections in role-play

Activity

◆ Create a supermarket in the role-play area and offer a selection of grocery items for the children to take into their supermarket.
◆ Ask the children to make a list of the things they would like to buy from the supermarket.
◆ Encourage the children to look carefully at the packaging and its words and pictures and then to take the items to their supermarket.
◆ Invite the children to read their list and shop in the supermarket.
◆ Give each child a basket or trolley and play money.
◆ Adults could play with the children to model reading shopping lists, finding items and paying at the till.

Extensions

◆ Make a trip to a supermarket.
◆ Explore what other information can be found on food packaging.
◆ Ask children to sort some shopping into hoops, for example by colour, shape or size.
◆ Find out which countries different items come from.
◆ Talk about the names of different shopkeepers: baker, pharmacist, butcher, etc.
◆ The children could make their own packaging for some items.
◆ Design and make a till to use in the home corner (see Supermarket till, pages 168–169).

Links to the Early Learning Goals

◆ Literacy: Reading, Writing
◆ Personal, social and emotional development: Making relationships
◆ Expressive arts and design: Being imaginative

Labels for supermarket

customer	shopkeeper
manager	groceries
fruit and vegetables	dairy
bakery	frozen foods
till	money
receipt	shopping list
purse	trolley

Play Activities for the Early Years
www.brilliantpublications.co.uk

Mother's/Father's Day card

Resources
Card; felt-tip pens; decorative items; Mother's/Father's Day card words (see page 120); Patterns sheet (see page 121)

Group size
Large groups

Learning objectives
◆ Using phonic knowledge to read and write simple, common words
◆ Handling mark making tools effectively
◆ Recognizing special events and customs observed by families
◆ Exploring creative and imaginative use of colour and design

Activity
◆ Talk to the children about Mother's/Father's Day and why we celebrate such days.
◆ Invite the children to make a card for their mother/father.
◆ Give each child a card and a copy of the Mother's/Father's Day card words sheet.
◆ Invite the children to decorate their cards as they wish. Some may possibly choose to draw pictures of their mothers or fathers and may like to use the words on the sheet to support them in writing 'My Mum' or 'My Dad'.
◆ Some children may like to take inspiration and ideas from the Patterns sheet when decorating their cards.
◆ Inside the card ask the children to use the sheet to help them write 'To Mum/Dad, I love you, from (name).'
◆ You may need to scribe for younger children.
◆ Show them how to use the sounds of letters (phonemes) to find the words they need.
◆ The children can take the finished cards home to give to their mother/father.

Extensions
◆ Use different materials to make cards, for example dried flowers, different fabrics, collage materials.
◆ Make cards for different purposes: birthdays, best friend, thank you, etc.
◆ Use a software package on the computer to make cards.
◆ Make envelopes to go with the cards.
◆ Use the patterns on the Patterns sheet to decorate different items: name labels, picture frames, etc.

Links to the Early Learning Goals
◆ Literacy: Reading, Writing
◆ Physical development: Moving and handling
◆ Understanding the world: People and communities
◆ Expressive arts and design: Exploring and using media and materials, Being imaginative

Mother's/Father's Day
card words

Happy Mother's Day	
Happy Father's Day	
to	Mum
Dad	I
love	you
from	with

Play Activities for the Early Years
www.brilliantpublications.co.uk

Patterns sheet

Name t-shirt

Resources

Plain t-shirt; non-toxic fabric pens; newspaper; masking tape; Patterns sheet (see page 121)

Group size

Small groups

Learning objectives

◆ Using memory and phonic knowledge to write names
◆ Handling a different medium to mark make effectively
◆ Exploring creative and imaginative use of colour and design
◆ Fine motor skills while handling equipment and tools

Activity

◆ Explain to children that they are going to design a t-shirt with their name on it.
◆ Lay the t-shirt flat on the table.
◆ Place a sheet of newspaper into the t-shirt to stop colour going through to the other side.
◆ To make it easier to write upon, fasten the t-shirt to the table using masking tape.
◆ Now ask children to write their name in the middle using the fabric pens. They can add patterns for decoration. The Patterns sheet provides some examples.
◆ Ensure the children are holding the pens correctly with a 'tripod' grip.
◆ Wash the t-shirts in a washing machine to set the colours.
◆ Let the children wear their t-shirts when they are dry.

Extensions

◆ Use different themes, for example my family, my pet, my favourite animal, holidays, my school.
◆ Use the Patterns sheet to decorate different items such as cards or frames.
◆ Design other pieces of clothing such as trousers, jackets, hats.
◆ Practise writing names on different items, for example door labels, coat peg labels, exercise books.
◆ Try writing with different tools, for example cotton buds, feathers, paint brushes.

Links to the Early Learning Goals

◆ Literacy: Writing
◆ Physical development: Moving and handling
◆ Expressive arts and design: Exploring and using media and materials

Play Activities for the Early Years
www.brilliantpublications.co.uk

Three-letter words

Resources
Empty yoghurt pots; Three-letter words sheet (see page 124); glue; scissors; workbooks (or paper); pencils; flip chart and pen

Group size
Small groups

Activity
◆ Photocopy the sheet. Cut out the pictures on the sheet and stick them onto the pots. Cut out the letters and place them in the pots.
◆ Give one pot to each child.
◆ Ask the children to look at the picture on their pot and say what it is.
◆ Now ask them to take the letters out of the pot and put them in the right order to spell the word that matches the picture, for example p-e-n for 'pen'.
◆ Help the children by explaining that they must try to say the word slowly and think of the sounds.
◆ When they think they have the correct order ask them to write the word in their workbook (or on a sheet of paper).
◆ When the children have finished ask them to swap their pot with someone else and to try another word. Carry on until each child has had all the pots.
◆ At the end go through all the words and write them on the flip chart.

Extensions
◆ Try the same activity with more complex words.
◆ Ask more able children to play this game verbally. For example, 'What word can you spell with the letters c, a, r?'
◆ Invite children to make words using wooden or plastic letters.
◆ Make greeting cards and encourage children to try to write simple messages (see Mother's/ Father's Day card, pages 119–121).
◆ Write sentences with missing words. Ask the children to try to fill in the missing word using phonics to work out the letters (see Finish the sentence, page 103).

Links to the Early Learning Goals
◆ Literacy: Reading, Writing
◆ Physical development: Moving and handling

Three-letter words sheet

	s	u	n
	p	e	n
	c	a	t
	p	i	g
	c	a	r
	e	g	g

Play Activities for the Early Years
www.brilliantpublications.co.uk

Mathematics

In the early years, mathematics needs to be practical and fun. Young children need to encounter mathematical concepts in their daily lives and in practical situations, which are meaningful to the children themselves. It is also vitally important that children enjoy using numbers and carefully planned games, stories, songs and play activities can all contribute to this.

Mathematics can be broken down into four main areas: number, space, shape and measurement. Within these areas children need to develop a number of skills including matching, sorting, counting, investigating patterns, making links and looking at relationships.

The activities in this chapter help children to:
◆   build a strong foundation and a positive attitude for future mathematical learning
◆   absorb practical mathematical concepts while having fun
◆   become confident in their understanding and use of numbers
◆   experience the properties of shapes, sizes and measures.

There are two Early Learning Goals (ELGs) within the specific area of Mathematics:

Numbers

Children count reliably with numbers from 1 to 20, place them in order and say which number is one more or one less than a given number. Using quantities and objects, they add and subtract two single-digit numbers and count on or back to find the answer. They solve problems, including doubling, halving and sharing.

Shape, space and measures

Children use everyday language to talk about size, weight, capacity, position, distance, time and money to compare quantities and objects and to solve problems. They recognize, create and describe patterns. They explore characteristics of everyday objects and shapes and use mathematical language to describe them.

The table on pages 126–127 shows which activities will help children to work towards, or achieve, these ELGs. Where an activity works towards ELGs in other areas, this has been indicated in the table.

Table of learning opportunities

Area	Aspect	Number carpet tiles (128–129)	Sand numbers (130)	Garden hoop count (131)	Shape pizza (132)	Sorting the laundry (133)	Message in a bottle (134–135)	Planting bulbs (136)	My foot (137)	Ten little monkeys (138–139)	Teddy bears' picnic (140)
Expressive Arts and Design	Being imaginative										✓
	Exploring and using media and materials									✓	
Understanding the World	Technology										
	The world			✓			✓	✓			
	People and communities					✓					
Mathematics	Shape, space and measures	✓			✓	✓		✓	✓		✓
	Numbers	✓	✓	✓	✓	✓	✓			✓	✓
Literacy	Writing										
	Reading						✓				
Personal, Social and Emotional Development	Making relationships										
	Managing feelings and behaviour										
	Self-confidence and self-awareness										
Physical Development	Health and self-care				✓						
	Moving and handling	✓	✓				✓	✓	✓		
Communication and Language	Speaking										
	Understanding										
	Listening and attention										

Play Activities for the Early Years
www.brilliantpublications.co.uk

Area	Aspect	Speckled frogs book (141–142)	More/less game (143–144)	Tidy up toys (145)	Cuddly toys in bed (146–147)	Fruit kebabs (148)	Butterfly pictures (149–150)	Cereal boxes (151)	Toy city (152)	Robot game (153)	Obstacle course (154)	The three bears (155)
Expressive Arts and Design	Being imaginative				✓				✓	✓	✓	✓
	Exploring and using media and materials	✓				✓	✓	✓				
Understanding the World	Technology											
	The world						✓					
	People and communities											
Mathematics	Shape, space and measures					✓	✓	✓	✓	✓	✓	✓
	Numbers	✓	✓	✓	✓							
Literacy	Writing											
	Reading											
Personal, Social and Emotional Development	Making relationships		✓		✓				✓	✓		
	Managing feelings and behaviour											
	Self-confidence and self-awareness											
Physical Development	Health and self-care					✓						
	Moving and handling			✓							✓	✓
Communication and Language	Speaking									✓		
	Understanding				✓				✓	✓		
	Listening and attention											

Number carpet tiles

Resources
Paints; paint brushes; 10 plain carpet tiles; Number cards (see page 129)

Group size
Small groups

Learning objectives
◆ Recognizing and remembering numbers 1 to 10
◆ Counting forward and backward
◆ Matching, sorting and comparing everyday objects
◆ Control and coordination in large and small movements

Activity
◆ Paint numbers 1–10 onto the tiles using brightly coloured paints to attract and interest the children. Leave to dry.
◆ In the outdoor area or in a large cleared space indoors, lay the tiles in a line, starting with 1 and finishing with 10. Ask the children to help you.
◆ Explain to the children that you would like them to jump from one number to the next, shouting out the numbers as they go.
◆ Make the jumping fun as children learn more when they are enjoying themselves.
◆ Now give each child a number card and ask them to place it on the matching number tile.
◆ Praise the children for each attempt.
◆ Finish the activity by collecting the tiles, counting backwards from 10 to 1.

Extensions
◆ This game can be developed further. For example, you could do counting on, counting back, counting in twos, fives, etc.
◆ Ask children to put the correct number of objects onto each carpet tile, for example five pencils on number 5.
◆ Play musical numbers. When the music stops the children have to jump onto a number – remove one tile and play the music again.
◆ Use the tiles for number songs and rhymes such as 'Ten Green Bottles', 'Ten Little Monkeys Jumping on the Bed', 'Ten Fat Sausages', 'Ten Currant Buns' (see Ten little monkeys, pages 138–139, and Speckled frogs book, pages 141–142).
◆ Suggest games, such as hopping four times on the number 4 tile or hopping back along the tiles while counting backwards from 10 to 1.

Links to the Early Learning Goals
◆ Mathematics: Numbers, Shape, space and measures
◆ Physical development: Moving and handling

Number cards

1	6
2	7
3	8
4	9
5	10

Sand numbers

Resources
Large pieces of card (eg A5 size); glue; pencils; sand

Group size
Small groups

Learning objectives
◆ Number names and number writing
◆ Ordering and counting skills
◆ The ability to learn through touch and tactile experiences
◆ Control and coordination in small movements

Activity
◆ Begin by explaining to the children that they are going to make some number cards.
◆ Write the numbers 1–10 on the cards.
◆ Ask the children to squeeze or paint glue onto the numbers and then sprinkle with the sand. You can add food colouring to the sand to make it more colourful.
◆ Once the cards are finished and dry, encourage the children to trace over the numbers with their fingers while you say what each one is. For example, 'This is number 1.'
◆ Ensure the children trace the numbers in the same direction they would normally write them.

Extensions
◆ Instead of sand you could use rice or cereal – anything with a texture (see Textured pictures, page 189).
◆ On the reverse side stick pictures of the appropriate number of objects. For example, for number 1 stick one bike, for number 2 stick two balls, etc.
◆ Encourage the children to look at the pictures so that they begin to relate the numerals to the quantities they represent. Using pictures of everyday objects provides a link between solid objects and mathematics.
◆ Ask the children to put the cards in the correct order from 1 to 10.
◆ Have a bowl of counters and ask the children to put the right number of counters on each card.
◆ Make another set of cards and play a game of Snap.
◆ Make some sand pictures (see Sand pictures, page 190).
◆ Invite children to try to identify numerals, made from plastic, foam or wood, just by feeling their shape. You could use a blindfold or put the numbers inside a bag.

Links to the Early Learning Goals
◆ Mathematics: Numbers
◆ Physical development: Moving and handling

Garden hoop count

Resources
Hoops; paper; pens

Group size
Small groups

Learning objectives
- Awareness of the environment and its similarities and differences
- Counting and addition skills
- Understanding of 'more' and 'less'
- Recording information in a chart
- Observational skills

Activity
- First give each child a hoop and ask them to place it anywhere in the outdoor area of the setting.
- Then ask them to guess how many leaves, flowers, ants, etc, they think they will find in the hoop.
- Record their guesses on a pictorial chart.
- Once they have guessed ask them to count how many there actually are. Record their findings on the chart.
- Ask the children to see if the number they guessed was more or less than the actual number, and by how many.
- Now do the same again but in a different part of the garden.

Extensions
- Count a variety of things: stones, leaves, twigs, berries, beetles, etc.
- Talk about the results found in different parts of the garden. For example, 'Why were there more flowers in one part than in another?'
- Show different ways of presenting results, for example bar charts, pie charts.
- Offer a similar activity in other locations, such as the seaside, park or town centre (see Trip to the park, page 177).
- Collect some items to use when making nature collages or mobiles (see Seaside collage, page 178, and Park collage, page 188).
- Find out more about the mini-beasts the children find (see Mini-beast safari, page 47).
- Write a list of all the things the children find.
- Discuss how the children can look after their local environment.

Links to the Early Learning Goals
- Mathematics: Numbers
- Understanding the world: The world

Shape pizza

Resources

1 pizza base; tomato puree; 3 rectangular pieces of ham; 4 circular pieces of tomato; 5 triangular pieces of cheese; 6 spherical olives; 7 triangular pieces of pineapple; 8 pieces of sweetcorn; baking tray; large plate; oven; knife

Group size

Small groups

Activity

◆ Begin by explaining to the children that they are going to make a pizza.
◆ Place the pizza base on a baking tray. Talk about the shape.
◆ Squeeze two oval squirts of tomato puree onto the base and ask, 'What shape is this?'
◆ Ask one child to spread the puree all over the base.
◆ Place the ingredients on a large plate and talk to the children about the different shapes. For example, 'What shape are the tomato slices?'
◆ Arrange the ingredients on the pizza, counting out the quantities.
◆ Bake in an oven at 220°C/425°F/gas mark 7 for 10 minutes. Cut up and enjoy.

Learning objectives

◆ Identifying and naming different 2D and 3D shapes and fractions
◆ Counting skills
◆ Recording information in a chart
◆ Understanding of healthy and unhealthy food choices

Extensions

◆ Encourage the children to not only look at the shapes but also feel them (using more than one sense enhances learning).
◆ Use a cardboard base and paper toppings to make an imaginary pizza.
◆ When cutting the pizza talk about halves and quarters.
◆ Make a salad and garlic bread to go with the pizza.
◆ Talk about healthy/unhealthy food (see Healthy food plate, page 58).
◆ Make a bar chart of the children's favourite pizza toppings.
◆ Write a shopping list of the ingredients.

Links to the Early Learning Goals

◆ Mathematics: Numbers, Shape, space and measures
◆ Physical development: Health and self-care

Sorting the laundry

Resources
Variety of newly washed laundry: socks, tops, trousers, dresses, etc

Group size
Whole class, then small groups

Learning objectives
◆ Comparing sizes, quantities, weights, textures and patterns
◆ Sorting and matching skills
◆ Counting everyday objects
◆ Recognizing and naming colours and familiar items

Activity
◆ Start by talking about laundry and how clothes are washed and then dried. Relate this to the children's own life experiences by asking them to think about who does the laundry in their homes and how it is sorted and put away.
◆ Lay out the clothes and ask children how they could sort them.
◆ Different ways of sorting could include:
  ❖ adult clothes, children's clothes
  ❖ by colour
  ❖ by item: all socks, all trousers, etc.
◆ Finally ask them which is the best way to sort out the laundry.

Extensions
◆ This activity could be used on different occasions:
  ❖ lunchtime – sort out the cutlery
  ❖ tidying up toys
  ❖ putting away the groceries.
◆ Count out the numbers of each type of clothing: 'How many socks are there?'
◆ Wash and dry some doll's clothes. Talk about how the clothes are washed and dried. Discuss how the water and soap clean the clothes and the sun and wind dry them.
◆ Encourage them to make comparisons between wet and dry clothes.
◆ Look at the different textures of the clothes and also the different patterns they can see (see Patterned jumper, pages 166–167).
◆ Read *Doing the Washing* by Sarah Garland (Puffin Playschool Books).

Links to the Early Learning Goals
◆ Mathematics: Numbers, Shape, space and measures
◆ Understanding the world: People and communities

Message in a bottle

Resources
Bottles of different sizes with lids; paddling pool; Messages sheet (see page 135); garden sticks; string; magnets and magnetic tape

Group size
Small groups

Learning objectives
- Recognizing and writing numbers
- Observing and identifying features in the environment
- Introduction to magnets and their properties
- Control and coordination in small movements
- Reading messages with help and support

Activity
- Begin by explaining to the children that they are going to make a game and then play it.
- Show children the 'outside' messages and ask them to put a different one in each bottle. Put the lids on the bottles.
- Now ask the children to paint a number (1–10) on each bottle.
- On the lid of each bottle put a small strip of magnetic tape.
- Invite children to make fishing rods by tying a magnet to a string and then attaching it to a garden stick.
- Fill up a paddling pool with water.
- Place the sealed bottles into the pool.
- Give each child a fishing rod and let them go fishing.
- When a child catches a bottle ask them what number it is.
- Help the child to read the message inside the bottle. Then support them in carrying out the task described in the message.

Extensions
- Other messages could ask children to find the biggest/smallest tree, plant, stone, bush, ball, leaf, toy, chair, etc.
- Introduce new vocabulary, such as 'big', 'bigger', 'biggest' and 'small', 'smaller', 'smallest'.
- To play the game indoors, fill a sink, bowl or tray with water, instead of a paddling pool, and use the 'inside' messages.
- Talk to the children about how the magnets stick to the bottles and let them find other things in the classroom that the magnets stick to.
- Decorate the bottles as boats.
- Discuss floating and sinking, and investigate.
- Use these ideas in a party game.

Links to Early Learning Goals
- Mathematics: Numbers
- Physical development: Moving and handling
- Literacy: Reading
- Understanding the world: The world

Messages sheet

Outside

Find the biggest flower and the smallest flower.

Find the biggest tree and the smallest tree.

Find the biggest stone and the smallest stone.

Find the biggest bush and the smallest bush.

Find the biggest stick and the smallest stick.

Find the biggest seed and the smallest seed.

Find the biggest paving stone and the smallest paving stone.

Find the biggest leaf and the smallest leaf.

Find the biggest conker and the smallest conker.

Find the biggest feather and the smallest feather.

Inside

Find the biggest book and the smallest book.

Find the biggest toy car and the smallest toy car.

Find the biggest chair and the smallest chair.

Find the biggest teddy bear and the smallest teddy bear.

Find the biggest doll and the smallest doll.

Find the biggest pencil and the smallest pencil.

Find the biggest pot and the smallest pot.

Find the biggest jigsaw and the smallest jigsaw.

Find the biggest bottle and the smallest bottle.

Find the biggest paint brush and the smallest paint brush.

Planting bulbs

Resources
Variety of plant pots; variety of bulbs; bag of compost; trowel; small bucket

Group size
Small groups

Learning objectives
◆ Solving practical problems using mathematical knowledge
◆ Understanding the practical meanings of words such as 'more'/'less', 'greater'/'smaller', 'heavier'/'lighter'
◆ Estimating, experimenting and verifying results – an important part of both mathematics and science

Activity
◆ Explain to the children that they are going to plant some bulbs.
◆ Lay out the plant pots according to size, from the biggest to the smallest.
◆ Ask the children to guess how many buckets would be needed to fill each pot.
◆ Record the guesses and then fill each one and see if the guesses were correct. Discuss which pot needed the most and which needed the least.
◆ Compare which pot is the heaviest and which is the lightest.
◆ Have a look at the bulbs and compare. Place them in order of size and then in order of weight (heaviest to lightest).
◆ Plant the bulbs in the pots, water them, then place them on the windowsill.
◆ Water regularly and let children observe how the plants grow.

Extensions
◆ Ask questions during the activity to encourage children to think carefully and to make connections and predictions: 'Which pot will hold the most compost? Which pot will hold the biggest number of bulbs? Is the pot heavier with or without compost? Which bulb is heavier/ lighter?'
◆ Ask the children to guess which bulb will grow to be the tallest plant. Label the pots with the children's guesses. Then record the growth over a number of weeks and see whose guess was correct.
◆ Discuss how the bulbs need water, compost and light in order to grow (see My own garden, page 163).
◆ Plant bulbs in different conditions. For example, you could grow one without water, one in the dark, etc.
◆ Discuss the similarities and differences between the plants grown.
◆ Name the parts of a plant.

Links to the Early Learning Goals
◆ Mathematics: Shape, space and measures
◆ Understanding the world: The world

Play Activities for the Early Years
www.brilliantpublications.co.uk

My foot

Resources
Paper; pencils; scissors; child's shoe; classroom items

Group size
Small groups

Learning objectives
◆ Ordering items by length
◆ Understanding the practical meanings of words such as 'longer' and 'shorter'
◆ Using parts of the body for measuring.
◆ Fine motor skills

Activity
◆ Discuss the terms 'longer' and 'shorter'. Show and talk about different items. For example, 'This pencil is shorter than this pencil.'
◆ Ask children to draw around their foot and cut it out.
◆ Now ask the children to look around the classroom for three items which are shorter than their foot.
◆ Then ask them to look for three items longer than their foot.
◆ Ask children to compare their foot cut-out to another child's. Is it longer or shorter?
◆ Finish by asking the children to put their foot cut-outs in a row from the shortest to the longest.

Extension
◆ Instead of a drawing round their foot children could draw round their hand.
◆ Do some feet or hand printing. Cut out the print and use it for measuring.
◆ Ask children to find items of different lengths in the classroom.
◆ Measure the children's heights and compare taller and shorter members of the group. Who is the tallest? Who is the shortest?
◆ Look at Mehndi patterns on feet and hands.

Links to the Early Learning Goals
◆ Mathematics: Shape, space and measures
◆ Physical development: Moving and handling

Ten little monkeys

Resources
Monkey sheet (see page 139); garden sticks; sticky tape; scissors; felt-tip pens; bed sheet; table

Group size
Large group

Learning objectives
- Understanding and using vocabulary for addition and subtraction
- Remembering numbers through singing and role-play
- Fine motor skills
- Creativity and imagination

Activity
- Give the children a copy of the Monkey sheet each and ask them to cut out the monkey and colour it in.
- Attach a garden stick to the back of the cut-out using sticky tape.
- Place a bed sheet on a table to represent the monkeys' bed.
- Ask the children to kneel behind the table and move the monkeys up and down so that the monkeys look as though they are jumping on the bed.
- Now ask the children to sing the song 'Ten Little Monkeys Jumping on the Bed' (see the Monkey sheet for the words).
- After each verse ask one child to remove their monkey.
- Ask the children questions: How many monkeys were on the bed? How many monkeys jumped off? How many monkeys are left?
- Carry on until there are no more monkeys left.

Extension
- Write numbers (1–10) on the monkeys.
- For younger children, only use five monkeys.
- For older children, adapt the song so that, instead of jumping off individually, they jump off in pairs.
- Attach an elastic string to the monkey cut-outs so they can be bounced up and down.
- In a PE lesson ask the children to pretend they are monkeys jumping on the bed. Use a trampoline or crash mat as a bed. Ask the children to act out the song.
- Use the monkeys for counting activities.
- Instead of monkeys use other items, such as frogs (see Speckled frogs book, pages 141–142).

Link to the Early Learning Goals
- Mathematics: Numbers
- Physical development: Moving and handling
- Expressive arts and design: Exploring and using media and materials

Monkey sheet

Ten Little Monkeys

Ten little monkeys jumping on the bed
One fell off and bumped his head.
Mummy called the doctor and the doctor said,
'No more monkeys jumping on the bed.'

Nine little monkeys jumping on the bed
One fell off and bumped his head.
Mummy called the doctor and the doctor said,
'No more monkeys jumping on the bed.'

Eight little monkeys jumping on the bed…

Teddy bears' picnic

Resources
5 cuddly teddy bears; tea set; food; picnic blanket

Group size
Small groups

Learning objectives
◆ Counting skills
◆ Understanding the practical meanings of words such as 'more' and 'less'
◆ Understanding and using addition and subtraction in an everyday situation
◆ Thinking visually

Activity
◆ Lay out the blanket and explain to the children that they are going to have a picnic with their teddy bears.
◆ Count out the teddies and place them around the blanket.
◆ Now count out some plates (ensure you start by only giving four).
◆ Give them out and ask:
  ❖ Are there enough plates?
  ❖ Do we need any more?
  ❖ How many more do we need?
◆ Now hand out the cups (start with only seven cups).
◆ Give them out and ask:
  ❖ Have we got enough cups?
  ❖ How many do we need?
  ❖ How many shall we take away?
◆ Share out the knives and forks while asking similar questions.
◆ When everything is laid out, give out the food and enjoy the picnic.

Extensions
◆ Involve children in similar activities when laying the table for lunch.
◆ The teddies can be used for other mathematical activities. For example, 'Which teddy is the tallest/oldest?'
◆ Sort the teddies into hoops by size, colour, etc.
◆ Ask the children to make a list of food for the picnic.
◆ Cook some food for the picnic: biscuits, cakes, sandwiches, etc (see Alphabet biscuits, pages 108–109, Chocolate rice snaps cakes, pages 32–33).
◆ Make up stories for the teddies.

Links to the Early Learning Goals
◆ Mathematics: Numbers, Shape, space and measures
◆ Expressive arts and design: Being imaginative

Speckled frogs book

Resources

Empty photo album (with peel-back plastic sheets); frogs cut from Speckled frogs sheet (see page 142) – each child will need at least 15 frogs; glue; pencil

Group size

Small groups

Activity

- ◆ Sing the song 'Five Little Speckled Frogs' with the children (see Speckled frogs sheet for words).
- ◆ Discuss with the children how to make a group book to accompany the song.
- ◆ Open the album and peel open the plastic sheet.
- ◆ Give each child a pile of frogs.
- ◆ Ask children to count out five frogs and stick them into the album.
- ◆ Write the numeral 5 underneath and seal the page.
- ◆ Next ask: 'If one frog jumps away how many will be left?' Use the frogs to help visualization.
- ◆ Use the terms 'take away' and 'one less'.
- ◆ Count out four frogs and stick them on the next page. Write the numeral 4 underneath.
- ◆ Carry on with this process until you get to zero.
- ◆ Finish the activity by singing the song again whilst looking at the book.

Learning objectives

- ◆ Counting skills
- ◆ Recognizing and writing numerals
- ◆ Understanding the practical meanings of 'one less' and 'one more'
- ◆ Remembering numbers through singing and role-play

Extensions

- ◆ By using a photo album with clear plastic you can use the book for number writing practice. The children can write over the numbers with a non-permanent felt-tip pen and then wipe clean to use again.
- ◆ Read the book from back to front to show the children how to count on 'one more' (see Ten little monkeys, pages 138–139, and Cuddly toys in bed, pages 146–147).
- ◆ Add other songs to the book. Possibilities include: 'Ten Green Bottles Sitting on a Wall', 'Ten in a Bed', 'Five Currant Buns in the Baker's Shop' and 'Five Fat Sausages'.
- ◆ Act out the song with the children pretending to be frogs.
- ◆ Look at the life cycle of frogs. If there is a local pond that children can visit, let them observe frogs as they develop.
- ◆ Make frogs by using a variety of art resources: clay, papier mâché, etc.
- ◆ Write a whole-class story about a frog.

Links to the Early Learning Goals

- ◆ Mathematics: Numbers
- ◆ Expressive arts and design: Exploring and using media and materials

Speckled frogs sheet

Five Little Speckled Frogs
Five little speckled frogs
Sat on a speckled log,
Eating some most delicious bugs,
Yum, yum.
One jumped into the pool,
Where it was nice and cool,
Now there are four speckled frogs,
Glug, glug.

Four little speckled frogs…

More/less game

Resources

Number cards sheet (see page 129) photocopied onto blue, red and green card and cut up to make three sets of cards; More/less die sheet (see page 144) photocopied onto card to make a more/less die; glue

Group size

Pairs

Activity

◆ Explain to children that they are going to play a card game. Ask the children to work in pairs.
◆ Lay out the red set of number cards face up on the table.
◆ Give the blue set of cards to child **A** and the green set of cards to child **B**. Both sets need to be in piles face down.
◆ Ask child **A** to turn over their top card and read the number.
◆ Next ask them to throw the die.
◆ If they get the side '1 more' explain that they have to choose a number from the red set which is 1 more than the number on their card. So, if they got 4 they need to pick number 5 from the red pack.
◆ Now put those cards to the side.
◆ Next it is child **B**'s turn to do the same.
◆ As the number of red cards decreases there will be occasions when a card cannot be picked as it has already gone.
◆ The game ends when all the red cards have gone.
◆ The winner is the one with the most red cards at the end.

Learning objectives

◆ Social skills such as cooperation and listening
◆ Counting skills and number recognition
◆ Understanding the practical meanings of 'one more' and 'one less'
◆ Understanding the meanings and significance of numbers.

Extensions

◆ Change the quantity on the dice, for example '2 more' and '2 less'.
◆ Let the children use counters to help them find the numbers they need.
◆ Use the die for other games.

Links to the Early Learning Goals

◆ Mathematics: Numbers
◆ Personal, social and emotional development: Making relationships

More/less die sheet

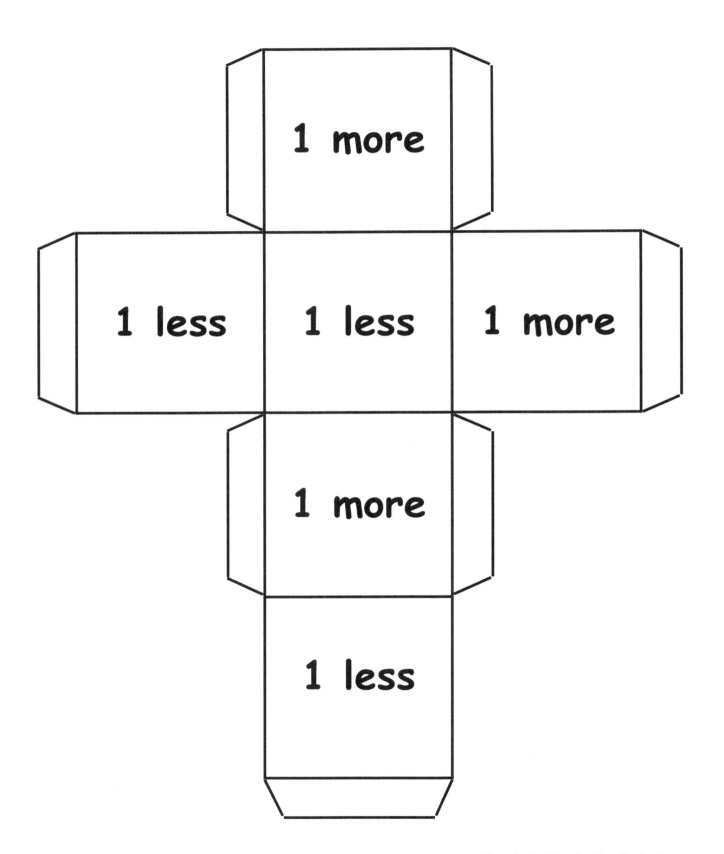

1 more

1 less   1 less   1 more

1 more

1 less

Play Activities for the Early Years
www.brilliantpublications.co.uk

Tidy up toys

Resources
A variety of small toys; toy box; flip chart and pen

Group size
Small groups

Learning objectives
◆ Understanding the practical meanings of 'one more' and 'one less'
◆ Counting skills
◆ Understanding how to express addition and subtraction in words

Activity
◆ Show the children the toy box and explain that you are going to hand out the toys one at a time.
◆ Start by giving each child one toy. Ask the children to count how many toys they have.
◆ Now give each child another toy and ask the children how many toys they have now.
◆ Write on the flip chart, 'Two is one more than one.' Read it aloud with the children.
◆ Underneath write, 'One add one is two.' Read aloud with the children again.
◆ Repeat the above until each child has ten toys.
◆ Allow the children time to play with their toys.
◆ Now explain to the children that it is tidy up time and that you need their help to put the toys back in the toy box.
◆ Ask the children to place their toys in a row and to count how many they have.
◆ Show the children the toy box and ask them to put one of their toys into it.
◆ Now ask them to count how many are left.
◆ Write on the flip chart, and ask children to read with you, 'Nine is one less than ten.'
◆ Underneath write, 'Ten take away one is nine.' Ask the children to read it with you.
◆ Repeat the above until all the toys are in the toy box. Thank the children for helping to tidy up.

Extensions
◆ For younger children, use just five toys.
◆ For older children add and take away two toys at a time.
◆ Repeat the activity with different resources such as balls and pots. Ask the children to place the balls in a pot one at a time using a spoon.
◆ Fasten number labels on the toys.
◆ Invite a group of children to stand together on a mat. Count how many children there are. Now ask the children to jump off the mat one at a time. Count how many children are left after each child has jumped.

Links to the Early Learning Goals
◆ Mathematics: Numbers
◆ Physical development: Moving and handling

Cuddly toys in bed

Resources

10 cuddly toys, 2 cardboard boxes; 2 doll's blankets or pieces of fabric; Cuddly toys in bed sheet (see page 147). (Photocopy the spinner onto card and cut out. Fasten pointer to spinner with split pin.)

Group size

Pairs

Activity

◆ Show the children the toys and explain that they are going to play a game with them.
◆ Encourage the children to make the boxes into beds for the toys and to add the blankets.
◆ Count out the toys and put five into one box and five into the other. Give each child a bed.
◆ The children take it in turns to spin the spinner.
◆ After each spin the child takes away the appropriate number of toys and counts how many are left.
◆ The winner is the one who has an empty bed first.

Learning objectives

◆ Understanding the practical meaning of subtraction.
◆ Creativity and imagination in role-play
◆ Following instructions and rules
◆ To think visually about subtraction
◆ Cooperation and taking turns

Extensions

◆ For older children, increase the number of toys in each bed to ten.
◆ Write down the results after each spin to give a more pictorial representation of the subtraction that has taken place.
◆ Back up the game by singing 'Ten in the Bed' (see sheet for words).
◆ Order the toys from the smallest to the biggest.
◆ Suggest to the children that they make the right sized bed and cover for each toy and support them in their attempts.
◆ Sort the toys into hoops, by colour, size or other criteria that the children think of.

Links to the Early Learning Goals

◆ Mathematics: Numbers
◆ Communication and language: Understanding
◆ Personal, social and emotional development: Making relationships
◆ Expressive arts and design: Being imaginative

Cuddly toys in bed sheet

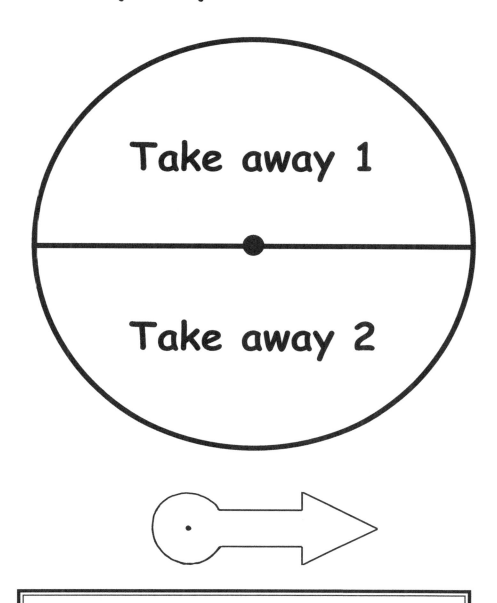

Take away 1

Take away 2

Ten in the Bed
There were ten in the the bed
And the little one said,
'Roll over, roll over.'
So they all rolled over
And one fell out
There were nine in the bed
And the little one said...

Continue until...
There was one in the bed
And the little one said,
'Thank goodness, peace at last.'

Fruit kebabs

Resources

Assorted fruit (seedless green grapes, bananas, red apples, oranges, melons, plums, etc); blunt knives; plates; dull-tipped kebab sticks

Group size

Small groups

Learning objectives

- Recording simple repetitive patterns
- Recognizing and naming familiar fruits
- Understanding and using shape names, new vocabulary and descriptive words
- Experiencing fruit through using a variety of senses, such as sight, touch, smell and taste
- Understanding healthy food choices

Activity

- Explain to children that they are going to make some fruit kebabs.
- Start by naming each of the fruits and talking about their colours, shapes and appearances.
- Cut the fruit into different shapes. Ask the children to help using blunt knives.
- When cutting the fruit use terms such as 'half' and 'quarter'.
- Show children how to make a simple repetitive pattern using the fruit, for example one banana, one orange.
- Now ask the children to form their own pattern with the fruit on a plate.
- Transfer this pattern onto the kebab sticks.
- Finish the activity by eating the resulting patterns.

Extensions

- Try using biscuit cutters instead of knives to cut up the fruit.
- Record the patterns by drawing them symbolically: for example, an orange circle for an orange segment and a yellow circle for a slice of banana.
- Make repetitive patterns with beads on strings or by printing with fruit.
- Invite children to wear blindfolds or close their eyes to guess what different fruits are by tasting them.
- Talk about the snack being very healthy (see Healthy food plate, page 58).

Links to the Early Learning Goals

- Mathematics: Shape, space and measures
- Physical development: Health and self-care
- Expressive arts and design: Exploring and using media and materials

Butterfly pictures

Resources
Butterfly template sheet (see page 150); paints; hand lenses; pictures of butterflies; brushes

Group size
Whole class, then small groups

Learning objectives
◆ Observational skills
◆ Recognizing patterns that occur in nature
◆ Designing and making creative patterns using paint
◆ Beginning to understand symmetry and balance

Activity
◆ Weather permitting, start by going for a walk in the garden/park to enable the children to see real butterflies. Use hand lenses to get a good look.
◆ Look at pictures of butterflies and talk about the patterns. Ask the children questions about the patterns they can see and whether they think all the wings are the same.
◆ Give each child a copy of the Butterfly template and explain that they can all paint patterns on the wings.
◆ Fold each butterfly shape in half and then open them up.
◆ Invite the children to paint a pattern on just one side.
◆ Fold the shapes in half again and press down firmly.
◆ Open out the papers and discuss the patterns that have been made.
◆ Finish the activity by displaying the butterflies.
◆ You could attach string to the butterflies and hang them from the ceiling.

Extensions
◆ Discuss the features of a butterfly: antennae, head, etc. When the paint is dry the children could add more features: feelers, body, etc.
◆ Find other patterns in nature.
◆ Ask children to design their own pattern.
◆ Make a pattern using beads and ask the children to copy it.
◆ Look at patterns in clothing (see Patterned jumper, pages 166–167).
◆ Remind the children that butterflies are small and delicate and they must be very careful when they are studying them.
◆ Explain the word 'symmetry' by looking at pictures of butterfly wings. Use mirrors to help the children understand.
◆ Read the book *The Very Hungry Caterpillar* by Eric Carle (Puffin Books). Find out about the life cycle of a butterfly (see The Very Hungry Caterpillar, page 194).

Links to the Early Learning Goals
◆ Mathematics: Shape, space and measures
◆ Understanding the world: The world
◆ Expressive arts and design: Exploring and using media and materials

Butterfly template sheet

Play Activities for the Early Years
www.brilliantpublications.co.uk

Cereal boxes

Resources
A variety of empty cereal boxes; glue; small sticky paper shapes

Group size
Small groups

Learning objectives
◆ 2D and 3D shape names
◆ Understanding that 3D shapes are created from 2D shapes
◆ Mathematical language to describe 3D shapes: such as 'faces' and 'corners'
◆ Fine motor control

Activity
◆ Give each child an empty cereal box.
◆ Explain that you would like them to unfold the box so it is flat.
◆ Help children with the unfolding to ensure there is no tearing.
◆ Once the box is flat ask children to count how many 2D shapes they can see. How many rectangles? How many triangles? etc.
◆ Ask children to count how many 2D shapes the box is made up of.
◆ Introduce words such as 'face', 'corner', 'edge'.
◆ Now ask the children to fold and glue to make a box again.
◆ Finish by decorating the box with some sticky paper shapes. The box can be used for storing items.

Extensions
◆ Older children could glue the boxes inside out to give a blank surface to decorate.
◆ Show how a cube is made up of six squares.
◆ Unfold other 3D shapes, for example a pyramid.
◆ Use 3D boxes to make a robot (see Robot game, page 153).
◆ Do some printing using a variety of 3D shapes.
◆ Use 2D and 3D objects, such as hoops, mats, tunnels and boxes, for role-play and physical play (see Obstacle course, page 154, and Going on a Bear Hunt, page 59).

Links to the Early Learning Goals
◆ Mathematics: Shape, space and measures
◆ Expressive arts and design: Exploring and using media and materials

Toy city

Resources

Variety of junk material (milk cartons, cereal boxes, egg boxes, bottles, and yoghurt pots); twigs; very large piece of cardboard; paint; paint brushes; paper; toy cars

Group size

Whole class, then small groups

Learning objectives

◆ Describing positions through mathematical language
◆ Teamwork, interacting and planning with others
◆ Listening, understanding and following instructions
◆ Visual/spatial intelligence and creativity

Activity

◆ This is a big project that can be spread over a number of days.
◆ Explain to the children that they are going to make a city for their toys.
◆ Begin by planning with the children how they are going to make their toy city.
◆ From the plan and the material available work with them to make the toy city. The city can be made on a large sheet of cardboard so that it can be tidied away if necessary.
◆ When complete, let the children use the toy cars to drive around the city.
◆ Ask the children to give you directions to get from one part of the city to another. For example, how can you get from the hospital to the school? The children may tell you to go forward and then turn left and then go under the bridge.
◆ Let the children have fun exploring their city.

Extensions

◆ Go for a walk in the local area. Point out key features such as the school, church, hospital, post box, etc (see Where we live, page 179).
◆ Use construction kits to make the toy city.
◆ Ask children how they get to school from their home. Record in writing for them.
◆ Play an opposites game. Ask: What is the opposite of forwards? What is the opposite of left? Play a game where every time you shout an instruction they have to do the opposite.
◆ Count how many items are in the toy city. How many houses? Cars? Roads?
◆ Make up a story about their toys in the toy city.
◆ Make a house for their favourite toy using junk material.

Links to the Early Learning Goals

◆ Mathematics: Shape, space and measures
◆ Communication and language: Understanding
◆ Personal, social and emotional development: Making relationships
◆ Expressive arts and design: Being imaginative

Robot game

Resources
A variety of junk material (cardboard boxes, egg boxes, bottles, tubes, cereal boxes, etc); sticky tape; paint; scissors; a gift/treasure (eg chocolate or a toy)

Group size
Pairs

Learning objectives
◆ Describing positions through mathematical language
◆ Teamwork, interacting and planning with others
◆ Listening and understanding, following and giving instructions
◆ Imitation, miming, acting and bodily awareness

Activity
◆ Explain to the children that they are going to play a robot game.
◆ Divide the children into pairs: one child is the robot and the other is the instructor.
◆ Ask the children to use the material provided to dress up one child as a robot.
◆ The instructor should then hide some treasure in the classroom whilst the robot closes its eyes.
◆ The instructor now gives the robot instructions so that it can find the treasure.
◆ When giving instructions ask children to use words such as: 'move forward three steps', 'turn left', 'go under the table', etc.
◆ The activity ends when the robot finds the treasure. The children could then swap roles.

Extensions
◆ Offer opportunities for movement and encourage children to pretend to be robots.
◆ Make up a story or poem about a robot.
◆ Ask children to think about what they would like a robot to do for them, for example clean up their room, or go shopping. Draw a picture of what it would look like.
◆ Count how many of each body part the robot has.

Links to the Early Learning Goals
◆ Mathematics: Shape, space and measures
◆ Communication and language: Understanding, Speaking
◆ Personal, social and emotional development: Making relationships
◆ Expressive arts and design: Being imaginative

Obstacle course

Resources

A map of the local area around the setting; climbing and balancing apparatus set up as an obstacle course

Group size

Whole class, then small groups

Activity

◆ Begin by looking at the map of the local area.
◆ Mark the location of the setting and point out key features, such as a post box, traffic lights, a bridge, etc.
◆ Discuss the ways that the children travel to the setting and the routes they take.
◆ Ask them to describe their journey – 'walk across the road', 'turn left', 'go over the bridge', etc.
◆ Show the children the apparatus.
◆ Invite the children to find many different ways of travelling over, under, through and around the apparatus.
◆ Encourage the children to describe what they are doing using words such as 'under', 'on', 'over', 'through'.
◆ Finish by choosing some children to demonstrate their work. Ask them to describe their actions as they do them.

Learning objectives

◆ Gross motor skills
◆ Creativity and imagination
◆ Opposites: over/under, up/down, etc
◆ Describing positions through mathematical language

Extensions

◆ Rearrange the equipment and ask children to find different ways of travelling (see Going on a Bear Hunt, page 59).
◆ Older children may be able to set up their own obstacle course.
◆ Count how many different ways they can travel on a piece of apparatus.
◆ Make a bar chart of the different ways the children travel to school, for example walk, car, bicycle.
◆ Ask children to draw a map of their route to school.
◆ Invite the children to make up an imaginary journey, for example to a treasure island.

Links to the Early Learning Goals

◆ Mathematics: Shape, space and measures
◆ Physical development: Moving and handling
◆ Expressive arts and design: Being imaginative

The three bears

Resources

Book: *Goldilocks and the Three Bears*; brown card; pencils; scissors; garden sticks; sticky tape; doll

Group size

Whole class, then small groups

Learning objectives

- Using mathematical knowledge of size to solve problems
- Ordering items by length
- Fine motor skills
- Listening to, remembering and retelling a story
- Describing positions through mathematical language

Activity

- Read the story *Goldilocks and the Three Bears*.
- Explain to the children that you would like them to make some bear puppets to go with the story.
- Give the children brown card and ask them to draw three bears. Remind them that one must be big, one must be medium and one must be small.
- Now ask them to cut out the bears and to check that they have bears of different sizes.
- Attach sticks to the backs of the bears using sticky tape.
- Now ask the children to use the bear puppets to retell the story. Use a doll for Goldilocks.

Extensions

- Encourage the children to make bowls, chairs and beds for the bears in three different sizes.
- Make a picnic for the bears and share the food.
- Make hats to fit the bears.
- Make a teddy bear picture using sticky paper shapes.
- Invite children to make some porridge. Measure the ingredients needed.
- Retell the story from the point of view of different characters (see I am Goldilocks / Baby Bear, pages 34–36).

Links to the Early Learning Goals

- Mathematics: Shape, space and measures
- Physical development: Moving and handling
- Expressive arts and design: Being imaginative

Understanding the World

Children are naturally curious and need opportunities to explore and investigate the world around them. They need help and support to develop knowledge and understanding, in order to make sense of their environment and its features. Practitioners can guide children as they explore the similarities and differences between people, communities, places, objects, materials, plants, animals and other living things. Technology now plays a large part in our lives and children can begin to learn, from a very young age, when and how to use it appropriately for particular purposes.

The activities in this chapter help children to:
◆ use their senses to explore the world, their local surroundings and key features
◆ develop observation skills, experiment and acquire new knowledge
◆ identify properties of plants, animals, materials and substances
◆ ask questions and acquire new knowledge
◆ predict, test theories, discuss conclusions and discover how things work
◆ use technology and specialized resources appropriately
◆ understand that they live in a multicultural society and value all people equally.

There are three Early Learning Goals (ELGs) within the specific area of Understanding the World:

People and communities
Children talk about past and present events in their own lives and in the lives of family members. They know that other children don't always enjoy the same things, and are sensitive to this. They know about similarities and differences between themselves and others, and among families, communities and traditions.

The world
Children know about similarities and differences in relation to places, objects, materials and living things. They talk about the features of their own immediate environment and how environments might vary from one another. They make observations of animals and plants and explain why some things occur, and talk about changes.

Technology
Children recognize that a range of technology is used in places such as homes and schools. They select and use technology for particular purposes.

The table on pages 157–158 shows which activities will help children to work towards, or achieve, these ELGs. Where an activity works towards ELGs in other areas, this has been indicated in the table.

Table of learning opportunities

Area	Learning opportunity	Kitchen utensil water play (159)	Chocolate birds' nests (160)	Sensory walk (161–162)	My own garden (163)	Butterfly costume (164)	Bird food (165)	Patterned jumper (166–167)	Supermarket till (168–169)	Make a house (170)	Body puppet (171–172)
Expressive Arts and Design	Being imaginative					✓		✓	✓	✓	
	Exploring and using media and materials	✓				✓			✓	✓	✓
Understanding the World	Technology								✓		
	The world	✓	✓	✓	✓	✓	✓	✓		✓	✓
	People and communities									✓	
Mathematics	Shape, space and measures	✓					✓				
	Numbers										
Literacy	Writing										
	Reading										
Personal, Social and Emotional Development	Making relationships								✓		
	Managing feelings and behaviour						✓				
	Self-confidence and self-awareness										
Physical Development	Health and self-care										
	Moving and handling	✓					✓		✓		
Communication and Language	Speaking			✓				✓			
	Understanding		✓		✓	✓					
	Listening and attention									✓	

Play Activities for the Early Years

www.brilliantpublications.co.uk

Area	Aspect	Interview the family	Me–past and present	Trip to the park	Seaside collage	Where we live	Pick a country	International music and dance	International food	Outdoor area
Expressive Arts and Design	Being imaginative			✔	✔	✔		✔		
	Exploring and using media and materials			✔	✔	✔		✔		
Understanding the World	Technology	✔								
	The world			✔	✔	✔				✔
	People and communities	✔	✔				✔	✔	✔	
Mathematics	Shape, space and measures					✔				
	Numbers									
Literacy	Writing									
	Reading						✔			
Personal, Social and Emotional Development	Making relationships	✔	✔	✔						
	Managing feelings and behaviour						✔			
	Self-confidence and self-awareness		✔	✔					✔	✔
Physical Development	Health and self-care								✔	
	Moving and handling							✔	✔	
Communication and Language	Speaking	✔	✔	✔	✔				✔	✔
	Understanding			✔	✔				✔	✔
	Listening and attention		✔	✔						
	Page no.	173–174	175–176	177	178	179	180–181	182	183–184	185

Play Activities for the Early Years
www.brilliantpublications.co.uk

Kitchen utensil water play

Resources

Water tray; water; a variety of kitchen utensils (sieves, egg beaters, spoons, bottles and jugs, bowls and beakers of various sizes)

Group size

Small groups

Learning objectives

◆ Similarities and differences between objects and materials
◆ Explaining why things happen and how things change
◆ Control and coordination in large and small movements
◆ Understanding of how liquids behave and their properties
◆ Understanding the mathematical concepts of size and volume
◆ Exploring and experimenting with materials and tools

Activity

◆ Fill the water tray with water.
◆ Provide the children with a wide selection of kitchen utensils.
◆ Let them explore and have some fun.
◆ Join in with children's play and conversation, modelling curiosity and finding out how water behaves as it is scooped, tipped and poured.
◆ Encourage the children to ask questions and help them to find the answers.
◆ Provide dishes of different sizes and encourage the children to guess which will hold the most water. Suggest ways that they might experiment to find out.

Extensions

◆ Provide other water play equipment such as water wheels, pumps and siphons.
◆ Add colouring or bubble bath or other safe substances to the water to change it.
◆ Introduce and explain the idea of items 'floating and sinking' and support children's investigations and experiments.
◆ Use sand instead of water and ask children to investigate its properties.

Links to the Early Learning Goals

◆ Understanding the world: The world
◆ Physical development: Moving and handling
◆ Mathematics: Shape, space and measures
◆ Expressive arts and design: Exploring and using media and materials

Chocolate birds' nests

Resources

Pictures, CD Roms or DVDs of birds and their nests; 1 chocolate bar; mixing bowl; hot water; box of corn flakes; 2 scooped orange halves; chocolate eggs; bowl and spoon

Group size

Small groups

Learning objectives

◆ Observing changes in materials and differences between liquids and solids
◆ Responding to an activity by asking relevant questions
◆ Understanding scientific processes, such as melting, freezing, heating and mixing
◆ Understanding opposites, such as hot/cold, soft/hard and wet/dry

Activity

◆ Invite children to look carefully at birds' nests, in pictures and on CD Roms or DVDs.
◆ Explain to children that they are going to make chocolate birds' nests.
◆ Break the chocolate into pieces.
◆ Put the pieces into a small bowl and melt over a bowl of hot water.
◆ Talk about how the chocolate changes.
◆ Pour in the corn flakes and mix.
◆ Pour the mixture into the orange skin halves.
◆ Place some chocolate eggs on top and place in the fridge.
◆ Ask the children to guess what will happen when the mixture has been put in the fridge.
◆ Once the mixture is hard remove from fridge and take the nests out of the orange halves.
◆ You now have your chocolate birds' nests. Eat and enjoy.

Extensions

◆ Let the children feel the ingredients before and after they have changed. Try heating the chocolate in a microwave oven instead, removing it at regular intervals to allow children to see the melting process as it happens.
◆ Talk to the children about how birds make nests.
◆ Ask the children to try to make a nest out of twigs or straw.
◆ Discuss how birds lay eggs and hatch their young.
◆ Discuss how children can encourage birds to come into their garden.
◆ Put out some bird food and try to identify the birds that come and eat it.
◆ Ask the children to design a bird table.

Links to the Early Learning Goals

◆ Understanding the world: The world
◆ Communication and language: Understanding

Sensory walk

Resources
Sensory walk sheet (see page 162); pencils; clipboards

Group size
Large groups

Learning objectives
◆ Observation and investigative skills
◆ Awareness of the senses and how to use them
◆ Fine motor skills

Activity
◆ Talk to the children about their senses: sight, hearing, touch, taste, smell.
◆ Show the children the Sensory walk sheet and explain that the pictures represent the senses of sight, hearing, touch and smell.
◆ Explain to the children that they are going for a sensory walk in the outside area and you would like them to use their senses (excluding taste).
◆ Ask children to draw on the sheet what they sensed. For example, in the smell box they could draw a flower; in the touch box they could draw the bark of a tree.
◆ Encourage children to share and discuss their findings with the group, either outside or after returning indoors.

Extensions
◆ Repeat the activity in other places, such as in the park or in an indoor area of the setting. Suggest to children that they might also like to try it at home or when out with their families.
◆ Investigate the sense of taste during snack time.
◆ Collect items to make a sensory collage (see Seaside collage, page 178).
◆ Ask children to investigate one object using as many of their senses as they can. For example, soap could be investigated using sight, touch and smell.
◆ Read *Spot's Walk in the Woods* by Eric Hill (Picture Puffins).

Links to the Early Learning Goals
◆ Understanding the world: The world
◆ Communication and language: Speaking

Sensory walk sheet

Play Activities for the Early Years
www.brilliantpublications.co.uk

My own garden

Resources
Area of ground prepared for planting; garden tools; seeds; long sheets of paper folded like concertinas to make zigzag books; pencils

Group size
Whole class, then small groups

Learning objectives
◆ Observation skills
◆ The growth cycle of a plant
◆ Names for the parts of a plant
◆ Conditions needed for growing plants

Activity
◆ Begin by showing the children the area of ground you will be using.
◆ Explain to the children that this is going to be their own garden.
◆ Encourage children to suggest and discuss plants that might be quick and easy to grow and involve them in buying the seeds.
◆ In small groups, plant some seeds and water them, explaining that the seeds will need soil, water and sunlight to help them to grow.
◆ Mark where each type of seed is planted.
◆ Organize a rota that allows all children opportunities to tend the seeds and the garden.
◆ Support children in recording the growth of their plants, weekly, in their zigzag books.
◆ Introduce new vocabulary to describe the plants, such as 'stems', 'leaves', 'roots', etc.
◆ Discuss similarities and differences between the plants.
◆ Let the children enjoy the fruits of their labour.

Extensions
◆ Compare the similarities and differences between different types of seeds.
◆ Plant the seeds in different conditions, for example, some without water, some in the dark.
◆ Sort some seeds into hoops according to size, colour, shape, etc.
◆ Make a collage using seeds.
◆ Count how many plants grow successfully and measure the tallest ones.
◆ Read *Jasper's Beanstalk* by Nick Butterworth and Mike Inkpen (Simon and Schuster).

Links to the Early Learning Goals
◆ Understanding the world: The world
◆ Communication and language: Understanding

Butterfly costume

Resources
Pictures of butterflies; strips of long card to fit around children's heads; pipe cleaners; card; sticky tape; party blowers; egg cartons; strips of card; crêpe paper; paint; paint brushes; felt-tip pens

Learning objectives
◆ Creativity and imagination
◆ Names for the parts of an insect
◆ Fine motor skills
◆ Observation of living things

Group size
Whole class, then small groups

Activity
◆ Share pictures of butterflies with the children and discuss their particular features, such as eyes, antennae, wings and long tongues.
◆ Invite children to make butterfly costumes.
◆ Support children in making, measuring and fastening headbands that fit their own heads.
◆ Offer resources, such as egg cartons, pipe cleaners, card and crêpe paper, for children to use as eyes, antennae, wings, etc.
◆ Now make the wings. Use coloured crêpe paper for the wings and attach card strip loops to go over their arms.
◆ Provide paints, pens and other media for decorating the headbands and wings.
◆ Encourage children to dress up in their butterfly costumes.
◆ Offer party blowers and invite children to pretend that they have long tongues like butterflies and can fly among the flowers, drinking their nectar.

Extensions
◆ Use the costumes for further imaginative role-play and drama
◆ Have a special butterfly party or mini-beast party where the children come dressed up as their favourite mini-beast.
◆ Make butterfly fairy cakes.
◆ Talk about symmetry by looking at butterfly wings (see Butterfly pictures, pages 149–150).
◆ Learn about the life cycle of a butterfly.

Links to the Early Learning Goals
◆ Understanding the world: The world
◆ Communication and language: Understanding
◆ Expressive arts and design: Exploring and using media and materials, Being imaginative

Bird food

Resources

Pictures of common birds; pine cones; peanut butter (NOTE: use warm lard instead if any child has a nut allergy); birdseed; string

Group size

Large groups

Learning objectives

◆ Observation skills
◆ Names for the parts and features of a bird
◆ Names of common birds and how to recognize them
◆ Appropriate behaviour and caring skills for interactions with living creatures

Activity

◆ Share pictures of common birds and their names with the children, and discuss their particular features, such as beaks, feathers, wings, etc.
◆ Ask the children how they could encourage birds to visit the outdoor area at the setting.
◆ Talk about the food birds eat: seeds, worms, etc.
◆ Explain how to make a treat for the birds to eat.
   ❖ First collect some pine cones.
   ❖ Spread some peanut butter over the pine cones and then roll the cones in a plate of birdseed.
   ❖ Tie a piece of string to the cones and hang them on a tree close to a low window that is easily accessible to the children.
◆ Ask the children to observe the birds that come to eat from the pine cones.
◆ Encourage the children to use the pictures of birds to try to identify them.

Extensions

◆ Make a bird table.
◆ Make some bird food by mixing warmed lard with birdseed, then leaving it to harden.
◆ Write a poem about birds.
◆ Take photographs and make a book about the birds that visit.
◆ Record some bird sounds with a tape recorder.
◆ Count the number of birds which come each day.

Links to the Early Learning Goals

◆ Understanding the world: The world
◆ Personal, social and emotional development: Managing feelings and behaviour

Patterned jumper

Resources
Items of clothing with patterns; Jumper outline sheet (see page 167); sponge shapes; paint; dolls or teddies

Group size
Large groups

Activity
◆ Show children the different items of clothing. Discuss the patterns on them and ask whether they can spot any repeating patterns.
◆ Give each child a copy of the Jumper outline sheet.
◆ Ask them to use sponge shapes to make a repeating pattern on the jumper.
◆ Leave the sheets to dry, then cut out the jumpers.
◆ Finish by sticking the jumpers on to some dolls or teddies and displaying them.

Learning objectives
◆ Observation skills and describing similarities and differences
◆ Recognizing, creating and describing patterns
◆ Fine motor skills

Extensions
◆ Ask children to bring in patterned clothing from home.
◆ Instead of sponge prints, use different items for printing, such as fruit, potatoes or utensils.
◆ Ask the children to make patterns on pieces of cloth using fabric paints.
◆ Make repeating patterns using beads and thread.
◆ Ask children to look for patterns in different objects in the classroom.
◆ Ask the children to look for patterns in nature, for example on butterfly wings (see Butterfly pictures, pages 149–150).

Links to the Early Learning Goals
◆ Understanding the world: The world
◆ Physical development: Moving and handling
◆ Mathematics: Shape, space and measures
◆ Expressive arts and design: Being imaginative

Jumper outline sheet

Supermarket till

Resources
Pictures or examples of tills; cardboard boxes; paper; paints; glue, sticky tape; scissors; supermarket role-play area (see pages 118 and 169 for labels); general grocery items (tins, bottles, cereal boxes, egg boxes, etc)

Group size
Whole class, then small groups

Learning objectives
◆ Creativity and imagination
◆ Using technology in their own environment
◆ Selecting and using appropriate resources for a creative project
◆ Listening and speaking skills through role-play
◆ Cooperation skills in group work

Activity
◆ Begin by making a trip to a supermarket.
◆ Draw the children's attention to all the electronic equipment used in the supermarket. For example, there are tills, bar-code scanners and automatic doors.
◆ If possible, arrange for the children to be allowed to touch a till and learn how one works. Explain how the food is scanned, show them a receipt and discuss how people pay with credit or debit cards.
◆ Back at the setting, provide pictures of tills or toy tills and encourage children to remember and look for their main features.
◆ Divide the children into small groups and ask them to construct a till using the materials provided. Give guidance and support where needed.
◆ Now use the till in role-play, encouraging children to take turns to be shop assistants and customers.

Extensions
◆ Investigate other electronic equipment used in a supermarket: weighing scales, bar-code scanners, etc.
◆ Ask children to write a shopping list (see Shopping at the Supermarket, pages 117-118 and labels, page 169).
◆ Find out which country different items come from.
◆ Talk about the different jobs people have in a supermarket: baker, pharmacist, butcher, etc.
◆ Adapt the role-play area to explore different shops in turn, such as a florist's shop, an optician and a bakery.
◆ Read *Going Shopping* by Sarah Garland (Atlantic Monthly Press).

Links to the Early Learning Goals
◆ Understanding the world: Technology
◆ Communication and language: Speaking
◆ Personal, social and emotional development: Making relationships
◆ Expressive arts and design: Exploring and using media and materials, Being imaginative

Food labels for supermarket

bread	cheese
milk	orange juice
chicken	chips
potatoes	cake
apples	biscuits
pears	meat
bananas	butter

Play Activities for the Early Years
www.brilliantpublications.co.uk
169
This page may be photocopied by the purchasing institution only.

Make a house

Resources

Book: *The Three Little Pigs*; pictures of houses; variety of different construction equipment (eg Lego®, Duplo®, wooden building blocks)

Group size

Large groups

Learning objectives

◆ Comparing different materials and their properties
◆ Features of a house
◆ Fine motor control
◆ Problem-solving

Activity

◆ Begin by reading the story *The Three Little Pigs*. Talk about the materials the pigs used and why the house of bricks was the strongest.
◆ Show the children pictures of houses and discuss the key features: roof, windows, door, etc.
◆ Show the children a variety of construction equipment.
◆ Now ask children to build a house using the construction equipment of their choice.
◆ Help the children to look at the house pictures for reference.
◆ When they have finished ask the children to be the wolf and try to blow their house down.
◆ Encourage children to adapt their designs to make their houses stronger.

Extensions

◆ Use different materials such as cardboard or wood to make houses.
◆ Look closely at the materials the pigs used and find out why the bricks made the strongest house.
◆ Look at pictures of different houses from around the world and investigate the materials used.
◆ Ask the children to look at the different types of houses they see when they go out, such as detached or terraced houses, flats or bungalows.
◆ If possible, visit a building site to see how bricks are used to make walls. A parent with brick-laying skills might be prepared to demonstrate how brick walls are made.
◆ Read *This is our House* by Michael Rosen (Candlewick Press).

Links to the Early Learning Goals

◆ Understanding the world: The world
◆ Communication and language: Listening and attention
◆ Expressive arts and design: Exploring and using media and materials, Being imaginative

Body puppet

Resources
Plastic skeleton; Body parts sheet photocopied onto card (see page 172); split pins; scissors

Group size
Small groups

Activity
- Ask the children to name the different parts of the body starting with the head and working down to the feet.
- Ask the children to move their arms and legs. Show a skeleton and point out the bones (joints) that help them to move.
- Explain to children that they are going to make a body puppet using the Body parts sheet and split pins.
- Give each child a copy of the sheet and ask them to cut out the body parts.
- Demonstrate how to use a split pin safely and ask children to join the body parts using the pins. Help where needed.
- When the puppets are finished let the children experiment with moving the different parts.

Learning objectives
- Names of body parts
- The order in which body parts fit together
- Understanding of how the body moves
- Fine motor skills

Extensions
- Ask children to bring in toys which have movable parts.
- Ask children to think of different ways to join the parts of the body.
- Sing the song 'Head, Shoulders, Knees and Toes'.
- Read *Head, Shoulders, Knees and Toes* by Annie Kubler (Child's Play International).
- Use puppets for role play or story-telling (see Puppet theatre, page 27).
- Invite the children to use scraps of fabric to dress up the puppets.

Links to the Early Learning Goals
- Understanding the world: People and communities, The world
- Physical development: Moving and handling
- Expressive arts and design: Exploring and using media and materials

Body parts sheet

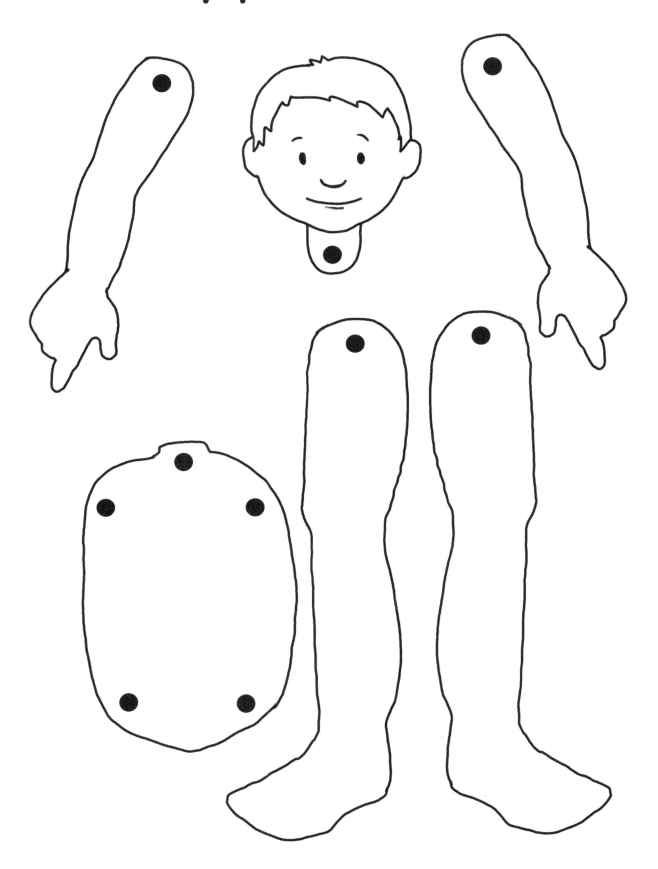

Play Activities for the Early Years
www.brilliantpublications.co.uk

Interview the family

Resources
Older members of the family; Questions sheet (see page 174); tape recorder; blank tape

Group size
Whole class, then individuals

Activity
- Begin by showing children a tape recorder. Explain how to operate it: turn on/off, rewind/ forward, and record.
- Ask the children how they could find out what schools and nurseries were like in the past.
- Discuss the types of people they could talk to and ask for their ideas.
- Explain that you would like them to interview and record an older member of their family talking about schools and nurseries in the past.
- Show them the Questions sheet and talk about the questions they could ask.
- Lend the tape recorder to each child in turn to take home.
- Once everyone has recorded their piece play the recording back to the class.
- Discuss with the children which things were similar/dissimilar to their school, preschool or nursery today. Which do they prefer?

Extensions
- Find out how old the setting's building is and how it has changed.
- Ask parents and grandparents to come in and talk to the children about their school days.
- Ask the children to find out about other things that have changed over time.

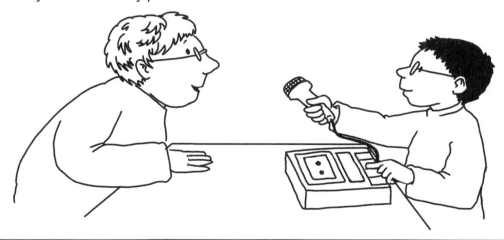

Links to the Early Learning Goals
- Understanding the world: People and communities, Technology
- Communication and language: Speaking
- Personal, social and emotional development: Making relationships

Questions sheet

How did you get to school?

What clothes did you wear?

What were your teachers like?

What did you eat for school dinners?

What was your favourite lesson?

Which games did you play in the playground?

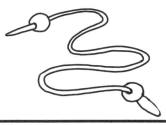

Play Activities for the Early Years
www.brilliantpublications.co.uk

Me – past and present

Resources
Photos of children when they were babies and now – doing different activities; Me sheet (see page 176); paper; pencils

Group size
Small groups

Learning objectives
- Observation skills
- Listening, speaking and discussion skills
- Understanding and comparing 'past', 'present' and 'future'
- Developing a positive image of themselves and respect and sensitivity for others

Activity
- Ask the children to bring photos from home, some from when they were babies and some from the present time.
- Give each child a copy of the Me sheet and explain the words 'past' and 'present'.
- Ask the children to stick their baby pictures on the past side and pictures from now on the present side.
- Gather the children together as a group to discuss their photos and the differences between past and present. Talk about different aspects, such as appearance and ability – when they were babies they crawled, now they can walk and run, etc.

Extensions
- Show children pictures of babies and invite them to guess who they are.
- Make a life line.
- Ask the children to draw a picture of what they think they will look like in the future.
- Ask the children to make a book about themselves.
- Show a variety of toys. Ask the children to sort them into baby toys and toys they could play with now.

Links to the Early Learning Goals
- Understanding the world: People and communities
- Communication and language: Listening and attention, Speaking
- Personal, social and emotional development: Self-confidence and self-awareness, Making relationships

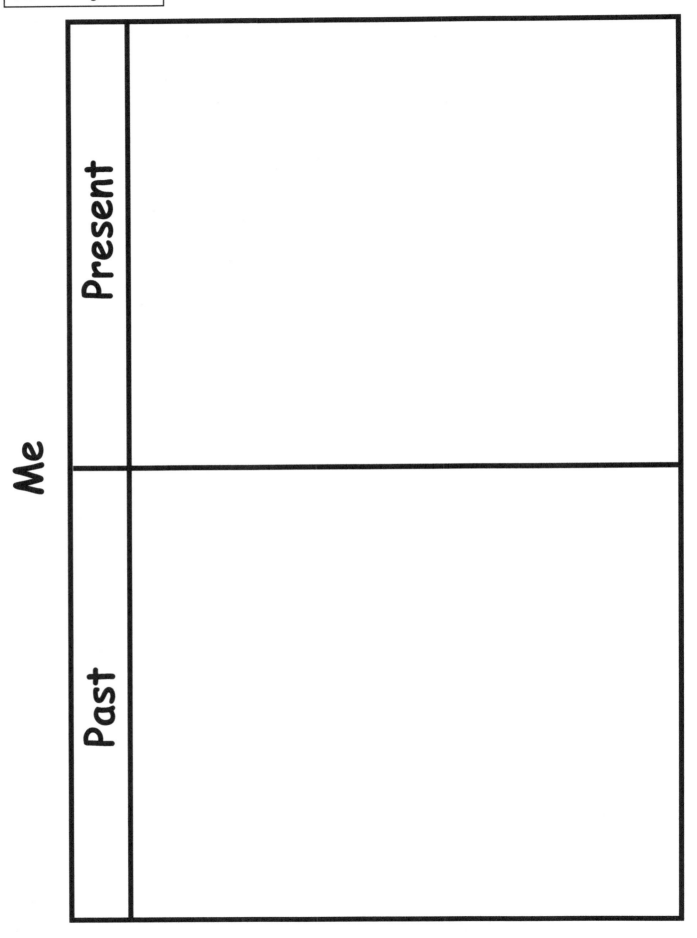

Me

Present

Past

Play Activities for the Early Years
www.brilliantpublications.co.uk

Trip to the park

Resources
Plastic bags; string; sticky tape; plastic coat hangers

Group size
Whole class

Learning objectives
◆ Observation of features in the local environment
◆ Problem-solving
◆ Creativity and imagination
◆ Fine motor skills
◆ Understanding of positive discussion of differing opinions, likes and dislikes

Activity
◆ Talk to the children about a trip to the park and explain that you would like them to collect some natural items such as leaves and twigs.
◆ At the park, encourage children to notice different features, such as trees, grass, flowers and the playground, model curiosity and explore and investigate with them.
◆ Collect a variety of items in bags to take back to the setting.
◆ After the outing, ask children what they observed at the park and what they liked or disliked.
◆ Offer the children coat hangers, sticky tape and string and support them as they construct 'park mobiles', using their collected items.
◆ Display all the mobiles.

Extensions
◆ Repeat the activity in other locations, such as the beach or the river, and compare the different types of items found.
◆ Go out in different seasons and find out how environments change throughout the year.
◆ Paint the items collected before attaching them to the hanger.
◆ Use the items collected in different art work, for example rubbings, prints or collage (see Park collage, page 188).
◆ Read *Spot Goes to the Park* by Eric Hill (Putnam Publishing Group).

Links to the Early Learning Goals
◆ Understanding the world: The world
◆ Communication and language: Listening and attention, Speaking
◆ Personal, social and emotional development: Self-confidence and self-awareness, Making relationships
◆ Expressive arts and design: Exploring and using media and materials, Being imaginative

Seaside collage

Resources
Pictures, CD-Roms or DVDs of the seaside; items collected from the seaside (shells, seaweed, pebbles, etc); card; glue

Group size
Whole class

Activity
- Plan a trip to the seaside or river.
- Ask the children to think about what they might see there.
- On the trip ask the children to collect different items for collage work, for example shells, seaweed, pebbles.
- After the outing, provide glue and card and invite children to make collages using the items they collected.
- Display the collages and discuss differences between the seaside or river location and the children's local environment.
- Discuss with the children what they like or dislike about the seaside or river and what they might like to change.

Learning objectives
- Observation of features in a variety of environments
- Creativity and imaginative design
- Awareness of caring for the environment

Extensions
- Offer this activity in various environments and compare the types of items found in different places (see Trip to the park, page 177).
- Use the items collected for other art activities such as printing or rubbing.
- Talk about ways of respecting and caring for the environment.
- Create a poem together, incorporating all the children's ideas.

Links to the Early Learning Goals
- Understanding the world: The world
- Communication and language: Understanding, Speaking
- Expressive arts and design: Exploring and using media and materials, Being imaginative

Where we live

Resources
Simple map of the local area; strips of card; small model buildings and small world toys (cars, people, trees, signs, etc)

Group size
Small groups

Learning objectives
- Observation and awareness of features in the local environment
- Understanding the concepts of position and distance
- Remembering and recreating familiar places and features from their own experience

Activity
- Take the children out for a walk around the local area. Encourage them to notice and describe familiar features and places, such as a post box, the doctor's surgery and the park.
- After the outing, share a simple map of the local area with the children.
- Explain to the children that you would like them to use the various resources to make a model of the local area.
- Offer strips of card and suggest that the children might like to use them to make roads.
- Provide small world buildings, cars and other toys and support the children in creating their own model of the local area, discussing the positions of familiar buildings such as the school, the hospital and the shops.
- Allow the children uninterrupted time to play freely with their model.

Extensions
- Use cardboard boxes to make model buildings.
- Use other materials to make different items for the model town.
- Ask the children to design an imaginary town (see Toy city, page 152).
- Count how many buildings there are.
- Ask the children to paint pictures of the things they saw on their walk.

Links to the Early Learning Goals
- Understanding the world: The world
- Communication and language: Understanding
- Mathematics: Shape, space and measures
- Expressive arts and design: Exploring and using media and materials, Being imaginative

Pick a country

Resources

Globe, magazines, pictures, books and CD-Roms about the chosen country; travel agency role-play area (see page 181 for labels); large poster-size paper and coloured pens

Group size

Whole class, then small groups

Learning objectives

◆ Knowledge and awareness of other countries of the world
◆ Understanding and awareness of different cultures, similarities and differences
◆ Working cooperatively as part of a group
◆ Gathering information from a variety of sources

Activity

◆ Begin by choosing a country for the week. You could spin a globe and ask a child to close their eyes and point to a country.
◆ Gather information with the children about the chosen country.
◆ Discuss the similarities and differences between the chosen country and the country the children live in.
◆ Divide the children into small groups and give each group a large sheet of paper.
◆ Explain that you would like the children to make a poster about the country for display in the travel agency role-play area. They can draw, or cut and stick pictures from magazines.
◆ Allow children uninterrupted time to play freely in the role-play area, encouraging them to take turns to be travel agents and customers.

Extensions

◆ Invite people who have lived in or visited the chosen country to come into the setting and talk to the children about it.
◆ Write a list of all the things the children would need to pack for a holiday in the chosen country.
◆ Make a travel brochure about the chosen country.
◆ Design a postcard that might be sent by someone on holiday in the chosen country.

Links to the Early Learning Goals

◆ Understanding the world: People and communities
◆ Personal, social and emotional development: Managing feelings and behaviour
◆ Literacy: Reading

Labels for travel agency

holidays	aeroplane
train	ferry
car	world map
countries	travel agent
customer	telephone
computer	travel brochure
tickets	suitcase

International music and dance

Resources
Tape recorder; recorded music from different countries to be played through a CD player, computer or other source (eg Spain – flamenco, India – bhangra, Caribbean – reggae, South America – tango); pictures/CD-Roms or DVDs of people doing the different dances

Group size
Whole class

Learning objectives
◆ Understanding and awareness of how different cultures use music and dance
◆ Knowledge and awareness of other countries and people of the world
◆ Gross motor skills, coordination and control of whole body movements
◆ Creativity and imagination

Activity
◆ Share music and pictures of dancers from different countries with the children.
◆ Discuss the children's different feelings when they hear the different types of music and invite them to move in ways that show their feelings.
◆ Model some simple dance moves appropriate to some of the pieces of music and encourage the children to copy them and make up others of their own.
◆ Play the pieces of music again and ask if children can remember or guess which countries they come from.

Extensions
◆ Make costumes to go with each type of music.
◆ Support children in finding out other information about some of the countries that the music comes from (see Pick a country, pages 180–181).
◆ Have a disco and play music from different countries.
◆ If possible, invite people into the setting to demonstrate the dances to the children.

Links to the Early Learning Goals
◆ Understanding the world: People and communities
◆ Physical development: Moving and handling
◆ Expressive arts and design: Exploring and using media and materials, Being imaginative

International food

Resources
Chapatti recipe sheet and ingredients (see page 184); aprons

Group size
Small groups

Learning objectives
◆ Understanding and awareness of traditional foods from different cultures
◆ Basic cookery skills
◆ Exploring different foods through the senses of touch, smell and taste
◆ Making decisions and expressing opinions effectively
◆ Discussing how different foods contribute to a healthy diet

Activity
◆ Introduce foods from different countries to the children through cookery activities and shared snack times. (Ensure that careful note is taken of any child's allergies, intolerances or cultural preferences before choosing and offering new foods.)
◆ Explain to the children that they are going to make some chapattis.
◆ Discuss that chapattis are eaten in India. Show pictures of Indian food.
◆ Ask the children if they have eaten Indian food before.
◆ Ask the children to wash their hands and put on aprons.
◆ Use the Chapatti recipe sheet. Involve the children in the cooking process as much as possible.
◆ Invite children to describe the taste and texture of the chapattis as they try them and to say whether they like or dislike them.
◆ Make foods from other countries with the children for snack times on other days.

Extensions
◆ Hold an international food day and arrange for the children to try a variety of different foods from countries around the world.
◆ Make a bar chart showing the children's favourite international foods.
◆ Read *Exploring Indian Food* by Sharukh Husain (Mantra Publishing) and *Lima's Red Hot Chilli* by David Mills (Aims International and Books Inc).
◆ Invite people from different communities into the setting to demonstrate how to make traditional foods from their cultures and to encourage the children to join in.
◆ Provide examples of the different utensils that people use to eat, such as knives, forks, spoons and chopsticks.

Links to the Early Learning Goals
◆ Understanding the world: People and communities
◆ Communication and language: Understanding, Speaking
◆ Physical development: Moving and handling, Health and self-care
◆ Personal, social and emotional development: Self-confidence and self-awareness

Chapatti recipe sheet

Ingredients
Chapatti flour
Rolling pin
Water
Butter

Resources
Sieve
Mixing bowl
Frying pan
Knife
Plate
Cup for measuring

Activity

1 Measure out 2 cups of chapatti flour and sift into a bowl. 	2 Add 1 cup of water slowly, mixing and kneading to make a soft dough. 
3 Take small pieces of dough and roll to form small balls, about the size of golf balls. 	4 Use a rolling pin to roll them out into a circle shape. 
5 Place a frying pan on the cooker until hot. 	6 Place a chapatti in the frying pan and cook on both sides. 
7 Turn it out onto a plate. Spread on some butter and let it cool. 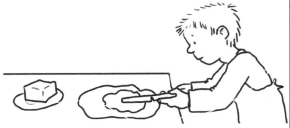	8 Cut the chapatti up into pieces for the children to eat. 

Play Activities for the Early Years
www.brilliantpublications.co.uk

Outdoor area

Resources

Any equipment required to fulfil children's ideas (paint, plants, bins, etc)

Group size

Whole class

Activity

◆ Walk around the outdoor area of the setting with the children.
◆ Talk with the children about their outdoor play area, what they like to do there and what they particularly like or dislike.
◆ Invite the children to suggest any additions and improvements that they would like to make to their outdoor area, such as keeping it tidier, painting some games on the ground or adding more resources.
◆ Help the children to make some of the changes they suggest.
◆ Walk around with the children again at a later date and discuss whether the changes have improved the outdoor area as planned.

Learning objectives

◆ Observation of features in the local environment
◆ Making decisions and expressing opinions and preferences effectively
◆ Awareness of caring for the environment

Extensions

◆ Ask the children to draw their own designs and ideas for their outdoor area.
◆ Talk about how the children could care for the environment.
◆ Ask the children to think of games they could play outside.
◆ Invite a caretaker or cleaner to come into the setting to talk to the children about how they keep buildings and equipment safe and clean.
◆ Encourage the children to contribute ideas and talk about feelings and behaviour, then make a list of basic rules together that will keep everybody safe and happy while playing outside.

Links to the Early Learning Goals

◆ Understanding the world: The world
◆ Communication and language: Understanding, Speaking
◆ Personal, social and emotional development: Self-confidence and self-awareness

Expressive Arts and Design

If they are encouraged and supported, children will use their imagination and creativity to present their own ideas and experiences using a wide range of media, including music and songs, mimes and gestures, movement and dance, paint and mark-making equipment, collage and model making, malleable materials, design and technology, role-play and drama, speeches, stories and rhymes.

Practitioners must offer children a wide variety of opportunities to express themselves creatively, to use and explore materials, tools and techniques and to develop imagination and confidence in the areas of art and design.

The activities in this chapter help children to:
◆ use their imagination in real-life and in make-believe scenarios and 'pretend' games
◆ respond positively and confidently to new experiences
◆ think independently and creatively
◆ use technology, tools, techniques and media appropriately.

There are two Early Learning Goals (ELGs) within the specific area of Expressive Arts and Design:

Exploring and using media and materials

Children sing songs, make music and dance, and experiment with ways of changing them. They safely use and explore a variety of materials, tools and techniques, experimenting with colour, design, texture, form and function.

Being imaginative

Children use what they have learnt about media and materials in original ways, thinking about uses and purposes. They represent their own ideas, thoughts and feelings through design and technology, art, music, dance, role-play and stories.

The table on pages 187 shows which activities will help children to work towards, or achieve, these ELGs. Where an activity works towards ELGs in other areas, this has been indicated in the table.

Table of learning opportunities

Area	Learning opportunity	Park collage (188)	Textured pictures (189)	Sand pictures (190)	Painting fun (191)	Guess the musical instrument (192)	Painting to music (193)	The Very Hungry Caterpillar (194)	Stained glass windows (195)	Feeling faces (196–197)	A snowy day (198–199)	Florist's shop (200–202)	Caterpillar fun (203)	Move to the music (204)
Expressive Arts and Design	Being imaginative	✓			✓		✓	✓	✓	✓	✓	✓	✓	✓
	Exploring and using media and materials		✓	✓	✓	✓	✓	✓	✓		✓		✓	✓
Understanding the World	Technology										✓	✓		
	The world	✓						✓			✓		✓	
	People and communities								✓			✓		
Mathematics	Shape, space and measures													
	Numbers													✓
Literacy	Writing											✓		
	Reading													
Personal, Social and Emotional Development	Making relationships											✓		
	Managing feelings and behaviour						✓			✓				
	Self-confidence and self-awareness	✓			✓						✓			
Physical Development	Health and self-care													
	Moving and handling			✓	✓			✓	✓		✓		✓	✓
Communication and Language	Speaking	✓			✓							✓		
	Understanding	✓	✓	✓			✓	✓	✓					
	Listening and attention					✓	✓	✓		✓				✓

Park collage

Resources
Plastic bags; card; glue

Group size
Whole class

Learning objectives
◆ Creativity and imagination
◆ Observation skills and using all their senses
◆ Group discussion and expressing opinions effectively

Activity
◆ Explain to the children that they are going on a trip to a park to collect different items such as leaves, twigs and stones for some collage work.
◆ During the trip encourage children to use all their senses. Ask them to smell the flowers; ask them to close their eyes and listen to what they can hear; ask them to feel the bark of a tree.
◆ After the outing, encourage the children to show each other what they have collected and to discuss colours, shapes and textures.
◆ Give each child a piece of card and ask them to make a collage using the things collected.
◆ Encourage the children to use their imagination.
◆ Encourage children to feel the collage pictures and try to identify some of the separate items without looking at them.

Extensions
◆ Use items collected for other art work, such as nature mobiles, 3D models, rubbings, and prints (see Trip to the park, page 177).
◆ Go for a mini-beast hunt in the park.
◆ Write a poem/story about the trip to the park.
◆ Count how many of the most popular items were collected.
◆ Make a book about the trip and illustrate it with some of the collected items.
◆ Read *Spot Goes to the Park* by Eric Hill (Putnam Publishing Group).

Links to the Early Learning Goals
◆ Expressive arts and design: Being imaginative
◆ Communication and language: Understanding, Speaking
◆ Personal, social and emotional development: Self-confidence and self-awareness
◆ Understanding the world: The world

Textured pictures

Resources
Clear glue; cardboard box; sand, salt and sawdust – all in shakers; paper; paint brushes

Group size
Large groups

Activity
◆ Invite the children to draw a simple picture. Choose a theme if it helps children to focus, for example a picture of the seaside.
◆ Ask the children to paint glue all over the picture.
◆ Now using the shakers show children how to shake sand, salt and sawdust onto different parts of the picture.
◆ Tip any surplus into a box.
◆ When the picture is dry, ask the children to feel it and talk about the different textures. Introduce descriptive words such as 'rough', 'smooth' and 'sharp'.

Extensions
◆ Invite children to feel the sand, salt and sawdust and to try to describe how they feel.
◆ Use sand, salt and sawdust in other art work.
◆ Mix sand, salt and sawdust with water and observe what happens.
◆ Find out how many cups of sand, salt or sawdust are needed to fill a selection of empty bottles and other containers.
◆ Allow the children some uninterrupted free play time to explore the materials.

Links to the Early Learning Goals
◆ Expressive arts and design: Exploring and using media and materials
◆ Communication and language: Understanding

Sand pictures

Resources
Cardboard; pencils; glue; water; paint brushes; coloured sand

Group size
Large groups

Learning objectives
◆ Fine motor skills and pincer grip
◆ Awareness of materials and their textures through the sense of touch
◆ Exploring colours, materials, equipment and resources
◆ Construction with malleable materials

Activity
◆ Explain to children that they are going to make pictures using sand.
◆ Give each child a piece of cardboard.
◆ Ask the children to draw a simple picture (large and not too detailed).
◆ Make a mixture of glue and water (about half as much water as glue).
◆ Ask the children to paint glue where they would like the first coloured sand to stick.
◆ Ask them to sprinkle sand onto that area. Leave it to dry and then shake or tap off excess sand into a box or tray.
◆ Now paint glue on a different area and sprinkle on a different colour.
◆ Repeat until the pictures are completed, then encourage children to touch the pictures and describe their textures.

Extensions
◆ Instead of sand use different materials such as sawdust, lentils, pasta shapes or dried beans (see Textured pictures, page 189).
◆ If you do not have coloured sands, use ordinary play sand and add powder paints or coloured glitter.
◆ Play with children in the sand tray or sandpit, with dry sand and after adding water, and talk about the properties of sand. For example, dry sand can be poured and does not retain its shape, but wet sand sticks together and can be used for modelling.
◆ Support children as they make sandcastles and other models from sand.

Links to the Early Learning Goals
◆ Expressive arts and design: Exploring and using media and materials
◆ Communication and language: Understanding
◆ Physical development: Moving and handling

Painting fun

Resources

Cotton buds, feathers, rollers, twigs, sticks, string, sponges, etc; paint; pots; paper; splash mat

Group size

Large groups

Learning objectives

◆ Fine motor skills and pincer grip
◆ Exploring and describing colours, materials, equipment and resources
◆ Making decisions and expressing opinions and preferences effectively

Activity

◆ Invite the children to participate in a group painting activity, using a wide variety of tools instead of paint brushes.
◆ Lay a splash mat on the floor.
◆ Pour some poster paint into the pots.
◆ Limit the number of colours to three or four to help the children to focus.
◆ Offer the children a choice of items to use for painting, that they may exchange whenever they wish.
◆ Give the children the paint pots and paper and let them paint.
◆ On your own paper demonstrate how to make dots and swirls using the various tools.
◆ Discuss with the children which items they most enjoyed painting with.
◆ Display the group picture, together with the tools and items that were used to make it.

Extensions

◆ Use different types of paint: watercolours, fabric paints, etc.
◆ Add things to the paint to make different textures: sand, sawdust, etc.
◆ Provide different types of paper to paint on: tissue paper, card, crêpe paper, etc.
◆ Invite the children to paint on different items: boxes, rocks, balloons, etc.
◆ Encourage the children to describe their work using a wide range of vocabulary.
◆ Invite the children to paint on a large scale using poster-size paper and large paint brushes.

SUSSEX DOWNS COLLEGE
LEWES LEARNING CENTRE

Links to the Early Learning Goals

◆ Expressive arts and design: Exploring and using media and materials, Being imaginative
◆ Communication and language: Speaking
◆ Physical development: Moving and handling
◆ Personal, social and emotional development: Self-confidence and self-awareness

Guess the musical instrument

Resources
A variety of musical instruments (eg drum, maraca, tambourine, and triangle)

Group size
Large groups and eventually whole class

Learning objectives
◆ Exploring and remembering the names and sounds of musical instruments
◆ Identifying different instruments and their sounds using only the sense of hearing
◆ Maintaining silence and concentration in order to listen and respond to sounds

Activity
◆ Invite the children to come together and sit in a circle.
◆ Begin by showing and naming each instrument.
◆ Play each instrument in turn to familiarize the children with the sounds.
◆ Place the instruments in the centre of the circle.
◆ Encourage the child to guess which instrument was played.
◆ Repeat the activity to allow all children to take turns at playing instruments and guessing them, if they wish to.

Extensions
◆ Play the game using household items that make sounds, instead of musical imstruments.
◆ Clap simple sound patterns and invite children to copy them using percussion instruments.
◆ Provide instruments for children to play as an accompaniment while they sing familiar songs.
◆ Use instruments to accompany a story.

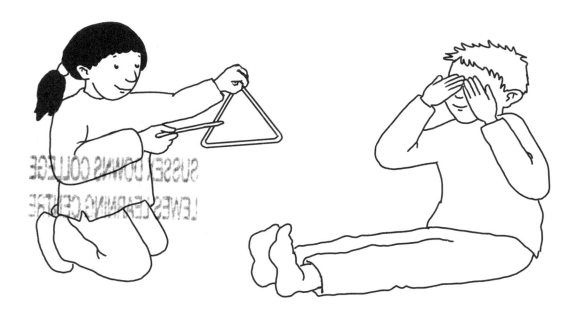

Links to the Early Learning Goals
◆ Expressive arts and design: Exploring and using media and materials
◆ Communication and language: Listening and attention

Painting to music

Resources

CD player or computer; paper; paints; paint brushes; two different pieces of music, one slow and downbeat, the other fast and upbeat

Group size

Whole class

Activity

◆ Ask the children to close their eyes and listen to some music.

◆ Play the first piece of music and ask them to think how it makes them feel. For example, discuss whether it might make them feel happy or sad, energetic or sleepy.

◆ Give each child a piece of paper and paints.

◆ Play the music again and ask children to paint how the music makes them feel, in whichever colours it makes them think of.

◆ Emphasize that the picture should not be of specific items. It should be of patterns and different colours.

◆ Now play the second piece of music and repeat the activity.

◆ Compare the two pictures and look for different colours and patterns.

◆ Encourage children to show their paintings to each other and spot any similar colours or patterns.

◆ Display the pairs of paintings with a label indicating the pieces of music that they were illustrating.

Learning objectives

◆ Listening skills
◆ Understanding different emotions expressed in music
◆ Expressing emotions creatively

Extensions

◆ Ask the children to compose a piece of music that makes them feel happy or sad.

◆ Talk about other emotions that are expressed in music.

◆ Play some music and ask the children to make movements inspired by the music (see Move to the music, page 204).

Links to the Early Learning Goals

◆ Expressive arts and design: Exploring and using media and materials, Being imaginative
◆ Communication and language: Listening and attention, Understanding
◆ Personal, social and emotional development: Managing feelings and behaviour

The Very Hungry Caterpillar

Resources
Storybook: *The Very Hungry Caterpillar* by Eric Carle (Puffin Books); musical instruments

Group size
Whole class

Learning objectives
- Attentive listening and concentration
- Creativity and imagination
- Names and sounds of a variety of instruments
- Life cycle of the caterpillar/butterfly
- Control and coordination in whole body movements

Activity
- Begin by reading the book *The Very Hungry Caterpillar*.
- Show the musical instruments. Name and play each one in turn.
- Read the story again and invite the children to make sounds with instruments to fit different parts of the story.
- Encourage children to play instruments appropriately as they listen to the story.
- Now ask the children to pretend they are the caterpillar and to act out each part as it is read. For example:
  - start as a ball on the floor for the beginning
  - slither on the floor like a caterpillar
  - eat the food and get fatter
  - roll up into a cocoon
  - fly away as a butterfly.
- Combine the role-play with the music, inviting children to take turns to make the sounds and to act out the story.

Extensions
- Make costumes and masks to go with the story (see Butterfly costume, page 164).
- Mount a display about the life cycle of a butterfly.
- Use a variety of art resources and different techniques to make caterpillars and butterflies.
- Repeat the activities to recreate the life cycles of other living things, such as frogs, chickens or sunflowers.
- Look at other mini-beasts and play instruments to express their movements.

Links to the Early Learning Goals
- Expressive arts and design: Exploring and using media and materials, Being imaginative
- Communication and language: Listening and attention, Understanding
- Physical development: Moving and handling
- Understanding the world: The world

Stained glass windows

Resources
Pictures of stained glass windows; thin paper; pencils; glue in a bottle with a pointed nozzle; crayons; felt-tip pens

Group size
Whole class

Learning objectives
◆ Observation skills
◆ Creativity and imagination
◆ Fine motor control
◆ Knowledge of communities and traditions

Activity
◆ Take the children to visit a local church.
◆ Encourage the children to observe using all their senses: look at the colours in the stained glass windows, smell the candles, listen to the organ, etc.
◆ After the outing, show the children pictures of stained glass windows.
◆ Discuss particular features of the windows with the children, such as the lines that break up the pictures, the bright colours and the effect created when the light shines through them.
◆ Explain to children that they are going to make some stained glass pictures.
◆ Support children in drawing simple pictures on thin paper, reminding them that the picture must be large enough and not too detailed (eg a house).
◆ Now ask them to draw lines to divide their drawings into pieces like stained glass windows.
◆ Squeeze lines of glue along the lines on the pictures, to outline each big shape, and leave them to dry.
◆ When the glue is dry, colour in each area with crayons or felt-tip pens.
◆ Display the pictures on windows, where the sun will shine through them.

Extensions
◆ Use different materials. For example, you could use strips of black paper for the lines and crêpe paper for the coloured pieces. Or use black paper with shapes cut out and stick coloured tissue paper pieces over the holes.
◆ Discuss the material used in real stained glass windows: lead, glass, etc.
◆ Discuss what a church is and what happens there.
◆ Look at other places of worship.
◆ Choose a stained glass window. Look at the picture and make up a story about it.
◆ Count how many stained glass windows were in the church.

Links to the Early Learning Goals
◆ Expressive arts and design: Exploring and using media and materials, Being imaginative
◆ Communication and language: Understanding
◆ Physical development: Moving and handling
◆ Understanding the world: People and communities

Feeling faces

Resources
Faces sheet (see page 197); cards with different scenarios

Group size
Whole class

Learning objectives
◆ Understanding and expressing own emotions
◆ Recognizing and understanding emotions in others
◆ Representing ideas and feelings through mime and role-play

Activity
◆ Begin by explaining to the children that you are going to show them pictures of faces showing different emotions, such as happy, sad and excited (see Faces sheet).
◆ Show a sad face and ask children to guess what the person is feeling. Ask them to think of different things that make them sad and to talk about these.
◆ Repeat the activity using other faces and emotions.
◆ Now explain to children that you are going to describe a situation and you want the children to show how they would feel. Possible scenarios include:
  ❖ you have lost your cat
  ❖ it is your birthday
  ❖ you are watching a scary film.
◆ Invite children to take turns to describe situations and model expressions.
◆ Model a variety of simple facial expressions for younger children to learn.
◆ Encourage older children to show how they would feel through expresssions, actions and movements.

Extensions
◆ Cut out pictures in magazines which show different expressions.
◆ Ask the children to make a book about things that make them happy, sad, angry, etc.
◆ Introduce a quiet area that children can use to sit and calm down if they feel sad or angry.
◆ Play a miming game, encouraging children to take turns to mime an emotion and to guess which one it is.
◆ Read *Copycat Faces* (Dorling Kindersley Publishing).

Links to the Early Learning Goals
◆ Expressive arts and design: Being imaginative
◆ Communication and language: Listening and attention
◆ Personal, social and emotional development: Managing feelings and behaviour

Faces sheet

A snowy day

Resources

Snowman templates (see page 199); cotton wool; buttons; twigs; paper; wool; glue

Group size

Whole class, then large groups

Activity

◆ Take children out for a walk on a snowy day.
◆ While out walking, encourage children to observe and experience the snow, using all of their senses. They may hold snow in their hands and pat it against their faces; look at the detail of snowflakes when they fall onto a dark surface or sleeve and how different the environment looks when covered in snow; let snowflakes fall into their mouths and melt there; smell the cold, fresh, icy air and listen to the snow crunching under their feet.
◆ If there is enough snow make a snowman.
◆ When the children are back indoors, offer them the snowman templates and assorted craft resources and invite them to make their own snowmen.
◆ Display the finished results for all to admire.

Learning objectives

◆ Awareness and observation through all of the senses
◆ Creative expression inspired by real experiences
◆ Fine motor skills

Extensions

◆ Watch the DVD *The Snowman* (Universal Pictures Video).
◆ Watch what happens to snow when it melts, then put it into a freezer and see what happens.
◆ Make a snowy day picture on the computer.
◆ Encourage children to make up stories about their snowmen and record them.
◆ Read *Zoe's Snowy Day* by Barbara Reid (Scholastic).

Links to the Early Learning Goals

◆ Expressive arts and design: Exploring and using media and materials, Being imaginative
◆ Physical development: Moving and handling
◆ Personal, social and emotional development: Self-confidence and self-awareness
◆ Understanding the world: The world, Technology

Snowman template

Florist's shop

Resources

Florist's shop role-play area (see pages 201–202 and 203 for labels); flowers made of a variety of materials (plastic, silk, paper, etc); baskets; pots; ribbon; tissue paper; till; play money; note pads; pens; play phone

Group size

Small groups

Activity

◆ Talk with children about a florist's shop and the different things the florist does, such as make bouquets, take telephone calls and deliver flowers.

◆ Talk about all the different occasions on which flowers may be given, such as birthdays, births of babies, Valentine's Day, anniveraries and funerals.

◆ Now invite the children to play in the florist's shop. Encourage them to take turns to be florists and customers.

◆ Play with the children and model the way a florist or a customer might behave, asking appropriate questions about a choice of flowers or where to deliver them.

Learning objectives

◆ Understanding real-life experiences through imaginative role-play
◆ Exploring people's thoughts and feelings in different situations
◆ Confident speaking, listening and cooperative play and interaction with others
◆ Attempting to write and record during play

Extensions

◆ Create other shops in the role-play area, such as an optician, a clothes shop, a supermarket, a shoe shop or a pet shop (see Hospital role-play pages 12–13 and Shopping at the supermarket pages 117–118).

◆ Encourage children to learn and remember their addresses and telephone numbers and to say them when ordering items in the shops.

◆ Support children in writing down names and addresses and other mark making.

◆ Make flowers using a variety of resources.

◆ Use play money to pay for the flowers.

Links to the Early Learning Goals

◆ Expressive arts and design: Being imaginative
◆ Communication and language: Speaking
◆ Personal, social and emotional development: Making relationships
◆ Literacy: Writing
◆ Understanding the world: People and communities, Technology

Labels for florist's shop 1

florist	customer
special offer	till
flowers for sale	open
pot	basket
seeds	soil
bouquets	telephone
Congratulations	Happy Birthday

Labels for florist's shop 2

Valentine's Day	For the birth of a baby
tulips 1p	daffodils 2p
lilies 3p	snowdrops 4p
roses 5p	carnations 6p

Play Activities for the Early Years
www.brilliantpublications.co.uk

Caterpillar fun

Resources

Pictures of caterpillars; for Caterpillar 1 – egg boxes, paint, glue, stapler and staples or masking tape, scissors, paint brushes; for Caterpillar 2 – cotton wool, stockings or tights, elastic bands, fabric paints, paint brushes; for Caterpillar 3 – Plasticine® and playdough

Learning objectives
- Creativity and imagination
- Fine motor skills
- Exploring the features of a caterpillar
- Using a wide range of resources and tools in art and craftwork

Group size

Whole class

Activity

- Share pictures of caterpillars with the children and discuss their particular features. For example, they have long bodies divided into segments and a variety of colours and patterns.
- Explain that they are going to make caterpillars using different materials:
  - ❖ **Caterpillar 1**
    Cut egg boxes into individual units, glue the pieces together in a long line and paint them, using pictures for ideas, then leave them to dry.
  - ❖ **Caterpillar 2**
    Stuff a stocking or one leg cut from a pair of tights with cotton wool, fasten it at intervals with elastic bands to make segments and paint it with fabric paints, using pictures for ideas.
  - ❖ **Caterpillar 3**
    Model the rolling of pieces of playdough or Plasticine® into long thin shapes to resemble caterpillars.
- Display all of the different caterpillars amongst real or paper leaves.

Extensions

- Read *The Crunching, Munching Caterpillar* by Sheridan Cain and Jack Tickle (Tiger Tales).
- Learn how the caterpillar changes into a butterfly.
- Make up a class story about a caterpillar (see *The Very Hungry Caterpillar*, page 194).

Links to the Early Learning Goals
- Expressive arts and design: Exploring and using media and materials, Being imaginative
- Physical development: Moving and handling
- Understanding the world: The world

Move to the music

Resources

CD-Roms or DVD of people dancing with different items (eg gymnasts dancing with ribbons); different types of music; ribbons; scarves; sticks; streamers; balls

Group size

Whole class

Learning objectives

◆ Control and coordination in whole body movements
◆ Understanding different emotions expressed in music
◆ Expressing emotions creatively

Activity

◆ Provide CD Roms or DVDs of people dancing with different items and watch with the children.
◆ Explain to the children that you are going to play some music and then ask them to move to it using different items.
◆ Play the music and ask them how the music makes them feel. Ask them how they could reflect these feelings in their movements.
◆ Give each child a ribbon and ask them how they could move to the music using the ribbon; for example, twirling around, running and trailing the ribbon behind them.
◆ Ask children to find a space. Now play the music again and ask them to move to the music using the ribbon.
◆ Model some movements or invite some of the children to demonstrate ideas if others seem unsure of what to do.
◆ Now play a different type of music and give children a different item (eg a scarf).
◆ Continue with the activity for as long as the children's interest lasts, offering them a variety of items to choose from, and making their favourite items accessible for free play.

Extension

◆ Make different items for the children to dance with, for example batons or streamers.
◆ Talk about different feelings and what makes the children feel happy /sad, etc (see Happy/ sad masks, pages 66–68 and Feeling faces, pages 196–197).
◆ Ask the children to use musical instruments to compose some music for other children to move to.
◆ Count how many different items the children dance with.

Links to the Early Learning Goals

◆ Expressive arts and design: Exploring and using media and materials, Being imaginative
◆ Communication and language: Listening and attention
◆ Physical development: Moving and handling
◆ Mathematics: Numbers

Complete Table of learning opportunities

Area	Learning opportunity	Listening area (10)	Toy telephone (11)	Hospital role-play (12–13)	I spy rhyming game (14)	Picture story (15)	Number rhymes (16–17)	The wheels on the fire engine (18)	Happy birthday (19)	Events of the day (20)	Copy my necklace (21)	Feely bag game (22)	What am I doing? (23–24)	My friend's weekend (25)	Food tasting (26)	Puppet theatre (27)
Expressive Arts and Design	Being imaginative	✓	✓	✓		✓	✓									✓
	Exploring and using media and materials							✓								✓
Understanding the World	Technology	✓														
	The world											✓			✓	
	People and communities								✓	✓				✓		
Mathematics	Shape, space and measures															
	Numbers															
Literacy	Writing			✓												
	Reading				✓											
Personal, Social and Emotional Development	Making relationships															
	Managing feelings and behaviour												✓			
	Self-confidence and self-awareness															
Physical Development	Health and self-care															
	Moving and handling										✓					
Communication and Language	Speaking		✓	✓		✓	✓		✓	✓			✓	✓	✓	
	Understanding				✓					✓	✓				✓	
	Listening and attention	✓			✓	✓	✓	✓	✓			✓	✓	✓		✓

Area	Skill	28	29–30	31	32–33	34–36	37	38	39–41	45	46	47	48	49	50	51	52	53
Expressive Arts and Design	Being imaginative	✓				✓			✓		✓	✓	✓					
	Exploring and using media and materials										✓							
Understanding the World	Technology						✓											
	The world																	
	People and communities																	
Mathematics	Shape, space and measures											✓						
	Numbers									✓	✓					✓	✓	✓
Literacy	Writing						✓	✓										
	Reading	✓				✓	✓											
Personal, Social and Emotional Development	Making relationships		✓	✓						✓	✓	✓	✓	✓	✓	✓	✓	
	Managing feelings and behaviour																	
	Self-confidence and self-awareness																	
Physical Development	Health and self-care														✓			
	Moving and handling				✓		✓	✓	✓	✓	✓	✓	✓	✓	✓	✓	✓	✓
Communication and Language	Speaking		✓	✓			✓	✓	✓									
	Understanding			✓	✓		✓		✓	✓	✓	✓	✓	✓	✓	✓	✓	✓
	Listening and attention	✓		✓	✓						✓	✓	✓	✓				✓
	Page no.	28	29–30	31	32–33	34–36	37	38	39–41	45	46	47	48	49	50	51	52	53
	Activity	Story of the week	Good manners certificate	Pass the teddy	Chocolate rice snaps cakes	I am Goldilocks/Baby Bear	Book about me	Diary	Make a maze	Chopstick challenge	Picnic food	Mini-beast safari	Bean bag games	Trolley dash	Traffic light game	Skittle fun	Easy catch	Musical cushions

Play Activities for the Early Years
www.brilliantpublications.co.uk

		Relation time	Is it healthy?	Healthy teeth	Healthy food plate	Going on a Bear Hunt	Grand Old Duke of York	Clay pot	Papier mâché ladybirds	Happy/sad masks	Find the hidden treasure	Guess the object	My favourite toy	Feel and guess	Making puppets	Sound game	Kim's game
Page no. →		54	55	56–57	58	59	60	61	62	66–68	69	70	71	72	73	74	75
Expressive Arts and Design	Being imaginative					✓	✓								✓		
	Exploring and using media and materials						✓	✓	✓		✓	✓					
Understanding the World	Technology																
	The world								✓		✓			✓			
	People and communities												✓				
Mathematics	Shape, space and measures																
	Numbers							✓	✓		✓						
Literacy	Writing											✓					
	Reading																
Personal, Social and Emotional Development	Making relationships					✓		✓					✓	✓	✓	✓	✓
	Managing feelings and behaviour									✓			✓	✓	✓		✓
	Self-confidence and self-awareness										✓	✓	✓	✓	✓	✓	✓
Physical Development	Health and self-care	✓	✓	✓	✓												
	Moving and handling	✓	✓	✓	✓	✓	✓	✓	✓								
Communication and Language	Speaking		✓	✓	✓	✓				✓	✓		✓		✓		
	Understanding	✓	✓	✓			✓	✓					✓	✓			
	Listening and attention	✓	✓	✓	✓	✓							✓		✓	✓	✓

Area	Aspect	Praise cards (76)	Happy family book (77)	Golden rules (78)	Crossing the road (79)	Special clothes (80)	Places of worship (81)	Pen pal class (82)	Being new (83)	Thank you cakes (84–85)	Parachute play (86–87)	The Boy Who Cried Wolf (88)	What is wrong? (89–90)	Nursery rhyme costumes (91)	Spider perseverance (92–93)	Sunflowers (94)
Expressive Arts and Design	Being imaginative	✓			✓				✓					✓	✓	
	Exploring and using media and materials									✓				✓		
Understanding the World	Technology							✓								
	The world															✓
	People and communities		✓			✓	✓	✓								
Mathematics	Shape, space and measures															
	Numbers															
Literacy	Writing							✓								
	Reading															
Personal, Social and Emotional Development	Making relationships	✓	✓	✓	✓	✓	✓	✓	✓	✓	✓	✓	✓	✓		✓
	Managing feelings and behaviour		✓	✓	✓		✓		✓	✓	✓	✓			✓	✓
	Self-confidence and self-awareness											✓				✓
Physical Development	Health and self-care				✓	✓				✓				✓	✓	
	Moving and handling										✓				✓	
Communication and Language	Speaking			✓			✓	✓	✓		✓		✓	✓	✓	
	Understanding								✓	✓	✓	✓	✓	✓	✓	
	Listening and attention	✓					✓		✓	✓	✓		✓	✓	✓	

Play Activities for the Early Years
www.brilliantpublications.co.uk

Area		Holiday times (95)	Festivals (96)	All about me (97)	Spider poem (101)	Favourite animals (102)	Finish the sentence (103)	Object game (104)	Same sound (105)	Snap (106–107)	Alphabet biscuits (108–109)	Letter of the week (110)	Word lotto (111–112)	Word search (113)	Mixed-up sentence (114)	Making a book (115)	Books from around the world (116)
Expressive Arts and Design	Being imaginative																
	Exploring and using media and materials																
Understanding the World	Technology									✓							
	The world	✓															
	People and communities	✓	✓	✓													✓
Mathematics	Shape, space and measures																
	Numbers											✓		✓			
Literacy	Writing				✓	✓	✓		✓		✓	✓			✓	✓	✓
	Reading	✓				✓	✓	✓		✓	✓		✓	✓	✓	✓	✓
Personal, Social and Emotional Development	Making relationships	✓	✓	✓													
	Managing feelings and behaviour																
	Self-confidence and self-awareness			✓				✓					✓			✓	
Physical Development	Health and self-care																
	Moving and handling				✓	✓	✓		✓		✓	✓			✓		
Communication and Language	Speaking			✓		✓											
	Understanding										✓						
	Listening and attention		✓	✓	✓		✓										

Activity	Page no.	Being imaginative	Exploring and using media and materials	Technology	The world	People and communities	Shape, space and measures	Numbers	Writing	Reading	Making relationships	Managing feelings and behaviour	Self-confidence and self-awareness	Health and self-care	Moving and handling	Speaking	Understanding	Listening and attention
		Expressive Arts and Design		**Understanding the World**			**Mathematics**		**Literacy**		**Personal, Social and Emotional Development**			**Physical Development**		**Communication and Language**		
Shopping at the supermarket	117–118	✓							✓	✓	✓							
Mother's/Father's Day card	119–121	✓	✓			✓			✓	✓					✓			
Name t-shirt	122		✓						✓						✓			
Three-letter words	123–124								✓	✓					✓			
Number carpet tiles	128–129						✓	✓							✓			
Sand numbers	130							✓							✓			
Garden hoop count	131				✓			✓										
Shape pizza	132						✓	✓						✓				
Sorting the laundry	133					✓	✓	✓										
Message in a bottle	134–135				✓			✓		✓					✓			
Planting bulbs	136				✓		✓											
My foot	137						✓								✓			
Ten little monkeys	138–139		✓					✓							✓			
Teddy bears' picnic	140	✓					✓	✓										
Speckled frogs book	141–142		✓					✓										

Play Activities for the Early Years
www.brilliantpublications.co.uk

Area	Aspect	More/less game (143–144)	Tidy up toys (145)	Cuddly toys in bed (146–147)	Fruit kebabs (148)	Butterfly pictures (149–150)	Cereal boxes (151)	Toy city (152)	Robot game (153)	Obstacle course (154)	The three bears (155)	Kitchen utensil water play (159)	Chocolate birds' nests (160)	Sensory walk (161–162)	My own garden (163)	Butterfly costume (164)
Expressive Arts and Design	Being imaginative			✓				✓	✓	✓	✓					✓
	Exploring and using media and materials				✓	✓	✓					✓				✓
Understanding the World	Technology															
	The world					✓						✓	✓	✓	✓	✓
	People and communities															
Mathematics	Shape, space and measures				✓	✓	✓	✓	✓	✓	✓	✓				
	Numbers	✓	✓	✓												
Literacy	Writing															
	Reading															
Personal, Social and Emotional Development	Making relationships	✓		✓				✓	✓							
	Managing feelings and behaviour															
	Self-confidence and self-awareness															
Physical Development	Health and self-care				✓											
	Moving and handling		✓							✓	✓	✓				
Communication and Language	Speaking								✓					✓		
	Understanding			✓				✓	✓				✓		✓	✓
	Listening and attention															

Play Activities for the Early Years
www.brilliantpublications.co.uk

211

This page may be photocopied by the purchasing institution only.

Area	Aspect	Bird food (165)	Patterned jumper (166–167)	Supermarket till (168–169)	Make a house (170)	Body puppet (171–172)	Interview the family (173–174)	Me–past and present (175–176)	Trip to the park (177)	Seaside collage (178)	Where we live (179)	Pick a country (180–181)	International music and dance (182)	International food (183–184)	Outdoor area (185)
Expressive Arts and Design	Being imaginative		✓	✓	✓				✓	✓	✓		✓		
	Exploring and using media and materials			✓	✓	✓			✓	✓	✓		✓		
Understanding the World	Technology			✓			✓								
	The world	✓	✓		✓	✓			✓	✓	✓				✓
	People and communities					✓	✓	✓				✓	✓	✓	
Mathematics	Shape, space and measures		✓								✓				
	Numbers														
Literacy	Writing														
	Reading											✓			
Personal, Social and Emotional Development	Making relationships			✓			✓	✓	✓						
	Managing feelings and behaviour	✓										✓			
	Self-confidence and self-awareness							✓	✓					✓	✓
Physical Development	Health and self-care													✓	
	Moving and handling		✓			✓							✓	✓	
Communication and Language	Speaking			✓			✓	✓	✓	✓				✓	✓
	Understanding									✓	✓			✓	✓
	Listening and attention				✓		✓	✓							

212

This page may be photocopied by the purchasing institution only.

Play Activities for the Early Years
www.brilliantpublications.co.uk

Area	Aspect	Park collage (188)	Textured pictures (189)	Sand pictures (190)	Painting fun (191)	Guess the musical instrument (192)	Painting to music (193)	The Very Hungry Caterpillar (194)	Stained glass windows (195)	Feeling faces (196–197)	A snowy day (198–199)	Florist's shop (200–202)	Caterpillar fun (203)	Move to the music (204)
Expressive Arts and Design	Being imaginative	✓			✓		✓	✓	✓	✓	✓	✓	✓	✓
	Exploring and using media and materials		✓	✓	✓	✓	✓	✓	✓		✓		✓	✓
Understanding the World	Technology										✓	✓		
	The world	✓						✓			✓		✓	
	People and communities								✓			✓		
Mathematics	Shape, space and measures													
	Numbers													✓
Literacy	Writing											✓		
	Reading													
Personal, Social and Emotional Development	Making relationships									✓				
	Managing feelings and behaviour						✓			✓				
	Self-confidence and self-awareness	✓			✓						✓			
Physical Development	Health and self-care													
	Moving and handling			✓	✓			✓	✓		✓		✓	✓
Communication and Language	Speaking	✓			✓							✓		
	Understanding	✓	✓	✓			✓	✓	✓					
	Listening and attention					✓	✓	✓		✓				✓

Play Activities for the Early Years
www.brilliantpublications.co.uk

213

This page may be photocopied by the purchasing institution only.

Lightning Source UK Ltd.
Milton Keynes UK
UKOW06f2043070914

238196UK00001B/2/P